# SELLING JESUS

## JESUS

**What's Wrong
with Marketing
the Church**

Douglas D.
Webster

INTERVARSITY PRESS
DOWNERS GROVE, ILLINOIS 60515

InterVarsity Press® is the book-publishing division of InterVarsity Christian Fellowship®, a student movement active on campus at hundreds of universities, colleges and schools of nursing in the United States of America, and a member movement of the International Fellowship of Evangelical Students. For information about local and regional activities, write Public Relations Dept., InterVarsity Christian Fellowship, 6400 Schroeder Rd., P.O. Box 7895, Madison, WI 53707-7895.

All Scripture quotations, unless otherwise indicated, are taken from the New Revised Standard Version of the Bible, copyright ©1989 by the Division of Christian Education of the National Council of the Churches of Christ in the USA and are used by permission.

ISBN 0-8308-1317-9

Printed in the United States of America ∞

**Library of Congress Cataloging-in-Publication Data**

Webster, Douglas D.
    Selling Jesus: what's wrong with marketing the church/Douglas
D. Webster.
      p.    cm.
    Includes bibliographical references.
    ISBN 0-8308-1317-9
    1. Church management.  2. Church growth.  I. Title.
BV652.W39  1992
254—dc20                           92-34516
                                        CIP

| 17 | 16 | 15 | 14 | 13 | 12 | 11 | 10 | 9 | 8 | 7 | 6 | 5 | 4 | 3 | 2 | 1 |
|----|----|----|----|----|----|----|----|----|----|----|----|----|----|----|----|----|
| 05 | 04 | 03 | 02 | 01 | 00 | 99 | 98 | 97 | 96 | 95 | 94 | 93 | 92 | | | |

*For Ginny*
*who insisted on it*

# PROMISES, PROMISES

There is a fine line between clever marketing and compromised spirituality.
GEORGE BARNA

A new genre of books has been hitting Christian bookstores: books on how to make your church a success. These books are promoted as "must" reading for pastors who want to be ready for the twenty-first century: "You too can discover the successful strategies and marketing tactics that will create a people flow to your church and promote a growth rate of ten percent annually."

The very idea that someone is laying it all out in black and white increases the pastor's heart rate as he buys the book on the church's account. "You won't be disappointed," says the bookstore manager; "this is one of our hottest releases."

Who doesn't want a leg up on the competition? No one wants to be left behind. These easy-reading books are products of the practical experience and innovative insights of Christian marketers, church-growth consultants and successful pastors.

Today's ecclesiastical visionaries come to the table with the latest psychographics, opinion polls and market research. They know what the people want: high-tech communications; high-touch pastoral care; laid-back, easy-flowing, eighteen-minute messages, just the right combination of anonymity and tender loving care; great child-care programs; multiple service options; ample parking; an upbeat, positive, exciting atmosphere; no pressure; plenty of meaningful intensity; and a warm, winsome, engaging pastor who can make you laugh and make you cry.

Today's user-friendly church is definitely not "your father's Oldsmobile." Gone are the acrimonious congregational meetings, interminable and irrelevant sermons, membership requirements to teach a class, ancient hymns, makeshift maintenance, potluck suppers with a lot of senior citizens at the head of the food line, evangelistic guilt trips, Wednesday-night prayer meetings and annual missions conferences.

Instead, there's a brand-new way of looking at church. Marketers are brimming with ideas on how your church can reach out to the "missing generation." The post-World War II baby boomer generation, representing a massive market share, is waiting to be tapped. They are turning forty, stressed out, bored with life, grasping for success, living for today, uncertain of the future, introspective, child-centered, health-conscious, sports-minded and looking for something more in life. The future-shock generation, nurtured in the culture of narcissism, is coming of age.

Disillusionment threatens. Diversions are expensive. Technology, mobility and the quest for success are poor defenses against divorce, cancer, parental failure and just plain emptiness. Comfort zones are cracking. Boomers are beginning to wake up to the fact that they have been living on a spiritual fault-line. Surface reality lacks foundation. Pleasant moments don't make up a meaningful philosophy of life. We still haven't found what we're looking for.

Enter the user-friendly church! Church-growth experts agree that the time is now for the church to meet market demand. It is America's only hope. The quest for transcendence is ripening, moral concern for our children's generation is growing, damaged emotions need relational care. Spirits need lifting. Broken hearts need healing.

There is a vast market out there for an evangelical product, but only churches that are market-sensitive and market-driven will be able to meet the baby boomer demand.

# 1
# CHURCH
# GROWTH
# MADE
# EASY

*That which we obtain too easily, we esteem too lightly.*
*It is dearness only which gives everything its value.*
*Heaven knows how to put a proper price on its goods.*
THOMAS PAINE

# If we are serious about the power of the Holy Spirit, we are going to be living constantly on the threshold of God's new and powerful work. We will not only have to live with change, ambiguity and opposition; we will *want* to—just as the early church did in Acts. The church was not meant to be a stagnant, tradition-bound institution but a dynamic, Christ-centered household of faith.

We wish to be neither sectarian nor shallow. Our desire is to be a household of faith under the lordship of Jesus Christ, by the power and love of the Spirit of truth, to the glory of God the Father.

The household of faith means for me a loving, serving, joyful congregation that is truly open to the powerful work of the Holy Spirit. This community expresses a quality of openness that reflects maturity, not indifference; it takes biblical integrity seriously, rather than casually, and passionately seeks spiritual vitality rather than cheap emotional hype. We want to tap the true drama of the gospel, which answers our quest for transcendence, the human need for significance and our longing for community. This calls for a tremendous work of spiritual discernment, humility and heartfelt prayer.

Such a biblical community can be seeker-sensitive without being consumer-oriented. It can make the gospel interesting without entertaining, and convicting without condemning. It can be both effective and faithful, serious and joyful, crossgenerational and mission-focused. It can redefine felt needs and meet spiritual needs. The household of faith is not a fun center or an escape from boredom, but a place of worship where the spiritual disciplines are modeled, the psalms are prayed and maturity is nurtured. It is a place where peer pressure, self-centeredness, anonymity and affluence are resisted. It is a community marked by the cross and blessed with resurrection hope.

### Marketing the Gospel

Is there a difference between building the church and marketing the church? Many sincere and thoughtful Christians are advocating a practical, market-sensitive, consumer-oriented approach to church growth. Their motives are unselfish and their goals righteous. They honestly want Christ to have an impact on American culture. The issue is not the Christian marketers' sincerity or integrity, but whether their strategies and tactics are consistent with a Spirit-led, Christ-centered approach to numerical growth and spiritual growth.

Professional marketer George Barna, a leader in popularizing church-growth marketing strategies, is a prolific writer. His books have become bestsellers: *Marketing the Church, The Frog in the Kettle* and *User Friendly Churches*. Other writers such as Leith Anderson in *Dying for Change* and Doug Murren in *The Baby Boomerang: Catching Baby Boomers As They Return to Church* share Barna's emphasis on churches' need to become more market-sensitive. In *An Inside Look at Ten of Today's Most Innovative Churches,* Elmer Towns illustrates many of Barna's principles of church growth by describing the fastest-growing market-driven churches in America.

Like the frog in the kettle, unaware of the danger of the steadily rising temperature, the church, Barna warns, is unaware that it's being eclipsed by the competition. He laments the fading impact of the church on secular culture. Oblivious to the deteriorating spiritual conditions of our country, the church is losing ground to the secular alternatives. The "encroachment of secularism" and the reversal of values from spiritual to material are catching us off guard. "Mesmerized by the lures of modern culture," the church is losing its spiritual edge.[1]

The solution Barna proposes is to radically change the American church's image and its philosophy of ministry. Having diagnosed the disease, Barna prescribes a full-blown marketing approach to help the church regain a positive influence on contemporary American culture.

Barna believes that the church's loss of influence can be reversed if we upgrade the quality of our performance, organize our programs to "optimize the time of the people" and use contemporary tools, such as computers, laser printers and FAX machines, to convince "those who are questioning Christianity that our faith is pertinent to the 21st century."[2] He advises setting up information systems that can handle inquiries with the speed we have grown accustomed to in customer service and employing an information-management specialist.

According to Barna, today's market-effective church will "shed existing attitudes of piety and solemnness, in favor of attitudes of anticipation, joy and fulfillment."³ The church must speak to felt needs, promote a positive attitude, aim for excellence and focus resources on their designated market niche. Sermons need to portray the Christian life as an attractive, relevant, compelling lifestyle.

These weekly "impact messages" should be delivered by multigifted, multitalented, take-charge leaders who grasp the vision of the church yet remain attuned to the details of church functioning. They are confident, flexible, effective pastors with the ability to delegate, the relational skills to interact and the entrepreneurial spirit to take advantage of great possibilities. They have the knack of being in the right place at the right time, lending their aura of authority to support other leaders and ministries in the church. They are described by Barna as practical, accountable, discerning people of God who spend much time in prayer.

Barna's prescription for growth and success includes all of the above and much more! His aim is to make every Christian a twenty-four-hour-a-day marketer. His promotional package is breathtakingly practical, motivational, entrepreneurial and spiritual. To hear him talk is to be almost convinced that Barna holds the key to the church of the twenty-first century. He has figured out what people want, what they need and how to give it to them.

## From Popular Opinion to Confession

One of the classic passages for understanding the church is Jesus' dialog with Peter in Matthew 16. Having retreated to Caesarea Philippi, Jesus apparently sensed that the time was right for some reflection on and analysis of his ministry with the disciples. The discussion began with Jesus' question to them, "Who do people say that the Son of Man is?" (v. 13).

Jesus' question was more an informal survey of popular views than a scientific public opinion poll. The disciples reviewed the more complimentary perspectives held by the general public: "Some say John the Baptist, but others Elijah, and still others Jeremiah or one of the prophets" (v. 14). They did not mention the hostile perspectives held by Jesus' enemies, such as the Pharisees. The result of this little poll demonstrated that Jesus had a pretty high rating among the people. More than just being popular, he was being taken seriously. He was right up there with the prophets.

From a publicist's standpoint, Jesus had both name recognition and a well-respected image. You might say he had market impact. He was in a position to capitalize on his popularity. No doubt this is what the disciples expected Jesus to do. Strategic marketing would have taken advantage of the situation by consolidating support and mapping out the next phase of the campaign.

The next question Jesus could have asked, if he'd had good marketing instincts, would have been, "How do we work this popular support to our advantage?" Or, "How do we build the disciple team?" Or even, "Does anyone have any ideas on how to handle the Pharisees and win them over?"

Instead, Jesus asked, "But what about you? Who do you say I am?"

It doesn't take a psychologist to see that this question implies a distinction between popular opinion and the position of the disciples. Jesus is deliberately aiming for a clarification. He is not satisfied with good PR and a strong position on the popularity index. His second question was designed to distinguish between popular opinion and personal conviction.

As happened so often, Peter spoke up for the disciples: "You are the Christ, the Son of the living God" (v. 16).

The difference between being one of the prophets and being the Messiah, the Son of the living God, is overwhelming. Peter is suggesting not simply a higher view of Jesus, but a radically different view of Jesus. The difference is not of degree but of kind.

Jesus is not one of many "key figures" in Jewish history, no matter how complimentary it might be to be likened to the prophets. Instead, Jesus is the culmination and climax of Jewish history—and of all history. He is the One all the prophets proclaimed and yearned to see.

Jesus asked his question to solidify the disciples' understanding. Instead of tuning in on the crowds' perceptions, he focused on the conviction of the disciples. The source for Peter's confession, Jesus claimed, was not human but divine. "Blessed are you, Simon son of Jonah! For flesh and blood has not revealed this to you, but my Father in heaven" (v. 17). Jesus did not take the credit for Peter's confession, but immediately called attention to the work of the Father.

Understanding the truth about Jesus was, and is, a matter of supernatural revelation. The power of persuasion lies not in human ingenuity and creativity, nor in techniques and methods, but in God's communication.

What follows has to be the most remarkable call to individuality and community ever given. "You are Peter, and on this rock I will build my church, and the gates of Hades will not prevail against it." This call comes not to the masses of people who feel positive about Jesus, but to the individual who confesses that Jesus is the Christ. The line between a complimentary view and a true confession is clearly drawn.

The church is not based on human opinions, no matter how positive. It is not an audience positively inclined toward Jesus, but a company of committed individuals whose lives depend upon the truth that Jesus Christ is Lord. The church must not obscure this truth by transforming a congregation into an audience, transforming proclamation into performance or transforming worship into entertainment.

The distinction between opinion and confession will be lost if the goal is mainly to attract more and more people to Jesus. Church attendance may grow, but true Christian individuality and community will be lost. If "unchurched Harry" feels perfectly at home in our churches, then chances are that we have no longer an authentic household of faith, but a popular cultural religion. We have a comfortable religion that makes practical sense to unconverted religionists like Nicodemus and secularists like the Samaritan woman. Rich young entrepreneurs are excited about our programs and Zacchaeus types are receiving therapy, but Jesus has never said to them, "You are ____, and upon this rock I will build my church." The line between positive opinion and true Spirit-led confession has never been crossed.

## Keys of the Kingdom

Following Peter's confession, Jesus makes a remarkable promise, which still stands as the greatest church growth promise ever made: "I will give you the keys of the kingdom of heaven, and whatever you bind on earth will be bound in heaven, and whatever you loose on earth will be loosed in heaven" (v. 20). Peter and all those who follow in his confession have the awesome responsibility of opening up the kingdom of God by proclaiming the life-changing, soul-saving, guilt-freeing word of eternal salvation.

By truly knowing, faithfully proclaiming and effectively living this truth, the church necessarily includes and excludes; it admits those who obey the will of God and rejects those who deny it. The keys of the kingdom symbolize knowing the will of God and applying God's truth. Marketing strategies, communication techniques and product packaging cannot make the keys of the kingdom more effective. It is faithfulness to the will of God that determines effectiveness.

The means and end of building the household of faith are distinctively ordained by God and not discovered through sociological analysis or psychological profiles. The latest trends and popular expectations do not change the church's agenda or alter its course. The church remains focused on eternal truths. It is sustained not by numbers or worldly recognition—which may in fact be detrimental to its effectiveness—but by the Word and Spirit of God.

If the church distinguishes between popular opinion about Jesus and the true confession of Christ and takes seriously the holy responsibility of the keys of the kingdom, it will be obvious that no choice has to be made between faithfulness and effectiveness or relevance and revelation. In the words of Stanley Hauerwas and William H. Willimon, the confessing church will seek

> to influence the world by being the church, that is, by being something the world is not and can never be, lacking the gift of faith and vision, which is ours in Christ. The confessing church seeks the visible church, a place, clearly visible to the world, in which people are faithful to their promises, love their enemies, tell the truth, honor the poor, suffer for righteousness, and thereby testify to the amazing community-creating power of God. The confessing church has no interest in withdrawing from the world, but it is not surprised when its witness evokes hostility from the world. . . . This church knows that its most credible form of witness (and the most "effective" thing it can do for the world) is the actual creation of a living, breathing, visible community of faith.[4]

## From Confession to Commitment

The only church built by Jesus is a confessing church. This is the only church that needs divine protection, and the only church empowered by God to engage the world with eternal direction. This is a totally unique, supernatural community.

Yet one important dimension remains to be explored in this strategic description of the church. Jesus' dialog with Peter affirms the confessional nature of the church and the supernatural wisdom and power of the church, but it does so by removing any tendency toward triumphalism. The confessing church will always be a church from below, an incarnational body, a community marked by the cross. The world will never see it as a success.

From the time of Peter's confession, Jesus began to talk about his death—how "he must go to Jerusalem and undergo great suffering at the hands of the elders and chief priests and scribes, and be killed, and on the third day be raised" (Mt 16:21). This kind of talk was out of line with Peter's expectations, just as it's out of line today with the dreams of many who advocate a marketing approach to church growth. Peter took Jesus aside and rebuked him: "God forbid it, Lord! This must never happen to you!"

Peter had gotten the confession right, thanks to the Spirit of God, but he had no idea how that confession was to be played out. He was laboring under an illusion. He was picturing a "successful" Messiah who had come to take charge, and Jesus was living out the role of the suffering Messiah. Jesus had come to lay down his life.

The Lord was not soft with Peter. In fact, his rebuke indicated the seriousness of Peter's heresy: "Get behind me, Satan! You are a stumbling block to me; for you are setting your mind not on divine things but on human things."

Peter can hardly be blamed for jumping to a false conclusion; many did the same thing, even after Jesus was nailed to the cross, and many still do. Their confession, like Peter's, is authentic, but their grasp of the commitment it entails gets lost in popular expectations, felt needs and religious ideas. They understand the cross doctrinally but not practically. They remember "Christ's death until he comes" when they celebrate the Lord's Table, but they do not understand the cross as a way of life. The cross does not shape their church-growth strategies and youth programs.

Like Peter, these people have conveniently divided confession and commitment. Some popular slogans reveal this polarization: "Christ is the answer," "Jesus saves," "God has a wonderful plan for your life."

The cross is regarded as a wonderful transaction between Jesus and God that enables us to find self-fulfillment, peace of mind and eternal life.

As Jesus found out with Peter, the cross is difficult to market. About the last thing Americans want to hear is a call to self-denial. But Jesus' first words to the disciples were "Follow me," and after his rebuke to Peter he clarified what it means to be a disciple: "If any want to become my followers, they must deny themselves and take up their cross and follow me" (Mt 16:24).

We are reluctant to follow Jesus' example. We'd rather base church growth on something else, something that will lure people in and get them involved before we say too much about commitment. But there is more to holding the keys of the kingdom than Peter realized—much more! Can church growth be made easy?

**Dialog and Discernment**

Many people genuinely can't imagine what would be inappropriate about applying marketing concepts and methodologies to all the ministries of the church. Marketing the church is as American as apple pie and baseball. If a marketing approach works for McDonald's and Disney World, it should work for evangelism and church growth.

If we're in the business of reaching people for Christ, why not take marketing strategies that have been proved successful among baby boomers and use them to help motivate this powerful and influential target audience to buy into the Christian faith? If polls and surveys tell us what turns Americans on, what's wrong with using that knowledge to turn the keys of the kingdom?

My purpose in this book is to open a dialog about one of the most important issues facing Christians in America. How do we present Christ to a consumer-oriented, sex-crazed, self-preoccupied, success-focused, technologically sophisticated, light-hearted, entertainment-centered culture? How do we strategize, as Jesus did with the disciples, to distinguish between popular opinion and Spirit-led confession? And how does the confessional church, as a community of Christian disciples, engage the world?

Many respected church consultants are offering straightforward, unambiguous answers. They are promoting strategies that encourage churches to establish a market niche, focus on a target audience, meet a wide range of felt needs, pursue corporate excellence, select a dynamic and personable leader and create a positive, upbeat, exciting atmosphere.

But are the Christian marketers asking the right questions? Is the issue for the American church authenticity *or* attractiveness, integrity *or* excitement? Judging from the answers given, the issue must be "how to create a people flow to your church." Or, what is the easiest, most effective, most efficient way possible to attract people, especially baby boomers, to Jesus Christ?

### Church Growth's Midlife Crisis

The nineteenth-century Danish Christian philosopher Søren Kierkegaard tells the story of his midlife crisis. Sitting at an outdoor café, he reflected on his comfortable, if not complacent, life. Everything was going well. His setting was idyllic, his mind totally relaxed. He was free from besetting pressures and physical hardship.

As he sat there, smoking a cigar, he began to daydream, musing inwardly about the purpose of his life.

"You are now," I said to myself, "on the way to becoming an old man, without being anything, and without really undertaking to do anything. On the other hand, wherever you look about you, in literature and life, you see the celebrated names and figures, the precious and much heralded men who are coming into prominence and are much talked about, the many benefactors of the age who know how to benefit mankind by making life easier and easier, some by railways, others by omnibuses and steamboats, others by telegraph, others by easily apprehended compendiums and short recitals of everything worth knowing, and finally the true benefactors of the age who by virtue of thought make spiritual existence systematically easier and easier, and yet more and more significant. And what are you doing?"[5]

Kierkegaard is not the first "midlifer" to think such thoughts, and certainly not the last. Among others, pastors, church-growth consultants, lay leaders and Christian market strategists occasionally think these thoughts too. "What can I do to make the church more relevant, more appealing? How can I make the Christian life both easier and more significant? How can we increase the impact of the church and give it more prominence?"

Those of us who want to introduce our neighbors to Christ feel these questions personally. "Am I living up to my potential for Christ? Doing my fair share for evangelism? Surely there is something more I can do for Christ to make the gospel more appealing . . . more compelling!"

Interrupting his self-communion just long enough to light another cigar, Kierkegaard was suddenly struck with a novel thought: "You must do something, but inasmuch as with your limited capacities it will be impossible to make anything easier than it has become, you must, with the same humanitarian enthusiasm as the others, undertake to make something harder."

This notion pleased Kierkegaard immensely. If everyone was trying to make life easier, maybe there was a need for someone like himself to make life harder. The time had come for some tension: some countervailing pressure to balance the pull in one direction.

As everyone tries to help make church growth easy, maybe it's time to make it difficult again. Are we working diligently to make the gospel so appealing and accommodating that we have forgotten how countercultural the kingdom of Christ really is? How do marketing strategies affect the impact of the gospel, the relevance of Christian proclamation, the integrity of the household of faith and the church's commitment to the whole counsel of God?

I wonder whether our quest for relevance needs to be in greater tension with faithfulness. Perhaps our preaching of the gospel has become too smooth, too predictable. We have tried so hard to package it for easy consumption that it no longer sounds like Jesus. We have become so practical that we no longer have anything to practice.

With so many consultants offering efficient, exciting strategies for marketing the church, maybe we need to re-examine our options. There is, after all, always a place for dialog over the integrity of our evangelism and the meaning of the church. Kierkegaard was right: "For when all combine in every way to make everything easier and easier, there remains only one possible danger, namely, that the easiness might become so great that it would be too great; then only one want is left, though not yet a felt want—that people will want difficulty."

These words remind me of a conversation I had with a group of Christians in Vancouver. At one time or another, each of them had chaired their church's leadership team. As you might guess, we quickly got into a discussion about the problems and blessings of working in the church.

There I was with ten church leaders, all actively committed to the work of the church, sitting around a table eating lunch and sharing their concerns and hopes for the church. Their very presence was a sign of strength, and their conversation reflected mutual respect.

I asked the youngest member, a lawyer in his thirties, whether he was committed to this body of believers for the long haul. Without a moment of hesitation he looked at me and said, "I'm a lifer. I can't leave when it's difficult. I am in it for life."

Lyle's conviction was shared by those around the table. They felt called to serve Christ and his body at the corner of West Eleventh Avenue and Sasamat Street. "A long obedience in the same direction" mattered more to them than public relations. They reminded me of the New Testament Christian communities described in Acts: struggling to remain faithful in a pagan culture, serious in their reflection on Christ and committed to sharing the gospel. Whatever else these spiritually minded deacons had learned about church growth, they knew it wasn't easy, and they had learned it was *God's* work.

When strategies for church growth are too secular, the presentation of the gospel too bland, the Christian life too easy and success too predictable, it's time to re-examine. Kierkegaard was onto something important:

> Out of love for mankind, and out of despair at my embarrassing situation, seeing that I had accomplished nothing and was unable to make anything easier than it had already been made, and moved by genuine interest in those who make everything easy, I conceived it my task to create difficulties everywhere.

# 2
# MARKETING
# THE
# CHURCH

This is truly an era in which the expression
"survival of the fittest" has meaning.
GEORGE BARNA

Handel's *Messiah* is the most
powerful oratorio ever written, and certainly one of the most popular.
Every Christmas, millions of people hear the Old Testament prophecies of the coming Messiah and are moved by the Christmas story
told in this great work. Handel's creative imagination set the biblical
account to music in a way that helps us "feel" the truth and prepare
our souls for worship. The recitatives and choruses echo in our hearts
long after the performance is over.

Most of us would assume that the Christian community of Handel's
day responded positively to this sacred oratorio upon its debut in
1742. But that was not the case. Handel faced stiff opposition from

sincere, thoughtful Christians who raised objections to his work.[1]

The criticism, which was to continue for nearly one hundred years, centered on the contention that Handel was profaning biblical truth— in other words, secularizing the sacred. Puritans objected to a performance of sacred truth in a theater with ticket sales, publicity and paid musicians. The message of the music was compromised, they claimed, by Handel's use of non-Christian musicians and soloists. For years Handel called his work simply a sacred oratorio, because many Christians felt strongly that it was a desecration of Christ for the word "Messiah" to be emblazoned on theater marquees.

One of Handel's critics was John Newton, the famous slave trader-turned-Puritan pastor who wrote the hymn "Amazing Grace." In a series of messages Newton expounded his opinion that if people simply read the Old Testament prophecies for themselves, they would get more out of the Scriptures than they would by listening to Handel's musical version. Newton also took issue with Handel's selection of passages, contending that Handel missed key truths because he did not include more Scripture.

It's hard for Christians today to imagine how anyone could have criticized Handel's *Messiah*. We're accustomed to paying twenty dollars a ticket to attend a "Christian" concert put on by a wealthy Christian performer whose music never mentions the Messiah or quotes from Scripture and makes perfect sense to many non-Christians as romantic love songs. Obviously we're far removed from nineteenth-century Puritan sensitivities.

When it comes to Handel's *Messiah,* it's easy to be critical of the critics. Why didn't the Puritans appreciate the tremendous evangelistic impact of this profound musical meditation on Christ's life? Originally Handel's "sacred oratorio" was especially conducive to worship because it was presented by small ensembles; this provided a musically precise, intimate listening experience, quite different from the grandiose productions put on by many of our churches today. Nevertheless, it was roundly criticized by the very people who should have been its strongest supporters.

We can admire the Puritans for being sensitive to biblical integrity and resisting anything that promoted the gospel as entertainment, but their criticism of Handel's *Messiah* carried important concerns too far. They rejected a new way of presenting the life of Christ because they felt it was tainted by a secular medium. Instead of rejoicing that God had gifted Handel to create a piece so powerful and biblical that the secular served the sacred rather than the other way around, these well-intentioned Puritans protested ardently.

The question raised by this historical case study is whether marketing the church, like Handel's music, is a God-given means for promoting the gospel or a cultural accommodation that compromises the gospel. Is there a danger of being overly sensitive to biblical integrity and authentic Christianity, so much that we resist a gift of the Spirit as the Puritans did? Are the tactics and strategies proposed by church marketers a case of the secular serving the sacred or the sacred serving the secular?

## The Power Team

Another case study may be helpful to clarify the issue. A few years ago, many of the churches in Bloomington, Indiana, were asked to support an evangelistic team coming to Indiana University's auditorium for several nights of outreach meetings. The group, known as "The Power Team," was made up of six young men who all weighed more than three hundred pounds. Large full-color posters carried images of their muscular builds and bulging biceps, and their tank tops boldly displayed the team motto, "The Power to Win." Their promotional publicity, designed to introduce the team to supporting churches, raved about how their crusades in other cities had succeeded in attracting thousands of young people. Local newspapers published articles about them, describing their workout routines and their daily diet of five meals totaling eight thousand calories.

This team of body builders was commended to the Christian community on the basis of how much they could bench press and the phenomenal amount of food they consumed to keep up their strength. Their evangelistic program consisted of smashing blocks of ice with their foreheads, carrying refrigerators on their backs, breaking baseball bats with their bare hands, snapping handcuffs and performing other feats of physical strength. Besides appealing for money to continue their evangelistic efforts, they used physical visual aids to give an extended invitation. They claimed that their ability to smash ice, break wood and bend steel was analogous to Christ's spiritual power over sin. "If you want this kind of power in your life, all you have to do is accept Jesus as your personal Savior. If you want the power to win in your life, come forward and receive Christ."

Hundreds did go forward, apparently providing evidence that Christ uses any means available to touch people's lives. Supporters of The Power Team claim that this approach reaches a certain segment of our culture that would never respond to an "intellectual" presentation of the gospel. They argue that many people need a visceral, graphic performance if they are to receive the "salvation invitation." Never mind the fact that the crusade took place on a university campus before thousands of college students, or that the physical feats were similar to the antics of a circus sideshow.

I wonder how our evangelical forebears, the Puritans, would have responded to this method of evangelism. If they thought the integrity and dignity of the gospel were compromised in Handel's *Messiah,* what would they think of the Power Team routine? Is the gospel of The Power Team presented with convicting, soul-searching power and a convincing call to commitment to Jesus Christ? Do those who respond to their clichéd invitation have any idea of who Jesus is and what it means to follow him?

American Christianity is increasingly tolerant of any and all methods, as long as they bring numerical results. We don't hear people praising the Lord because millions of people watch the NFL Super Bowl, but if five thousand people attend church it must be God's doing. We have virtually eliminated discernment of the will of God—and sadly, that's the equivalent of losing the keys of the kingdom.

Anything goes as long as it is defended for the sake of evangelism or promotes church growth. The single most decisive support for new methods is popularity. If people are buying, the product must be good. Public opinion has become an arbiter of truth, dictating the terms of acceptability according to the marketplace. The sovereignty of the audience makes serious, prayerful thinking about the will of God unnecessary, because opinions are formed on the basis of taste and preferences rather than careful biblical conviction and thoughtful theological reflection. Americans easily become "slaves of slogans" when discernment is reduced to ratings.[2]

**Discernment**

The apostle Paul's concern for the believers at Philippi is equally appropriate for the American church. "This is my prayer," Paul writes, "that your love may overflow more and more with knowledge and full insight to help you to determine what is best, so that in the day of Christ you may be pure and blameless, having produced the harvest of righteousness that comes through Jesus Christ for the glory and praise of God" (Phil 1:9-11).

The loving thing to do is not what public opinion dictates, but what the Word of God commands as the Spirit of God leads. This understanding is not facilitated by polls and surveys but by prayerful dependence upon God, humble service, patient learning, true Christian friendship and genuine worship.

Instead of describing love as an emotional response to culturally induced felt needs, Paul characterized it in terms of in-depth insight, moral purity and ethical sensitivity. For Paul, the loving congregation was by definition a wise congregation, sensitive to the purity and holiness of God and the integrity of the gospel. Love for Christ and his body required discerning between proclamation and propaganda, challenge and manipulation, spiritual growth and empire building, faithfulness and worldly success.

Love for Christ distinguishes a congregation from an audience and spiritual needs from felt needs. Love discerns between religious tour guides and pioneers in the faith, and it wisely distinguishes true pastors from performers. Love overcomes judgmental attitudes toward new works of the Holy Spirit, such as Handel's *Messiah,* but love also discerns The Power Team's shallow trivialization of the gospel.

**What Is Marketing?**
It may be best to let America's foremost church marketer, George Barna, define what he means by marketing the church:

Marketing . . . involves a broad range of activities such as research, product positioning, awareness development, strategic planning, pricing, advertising, public relations, and audience segmentation. . . . the basic thrust of marketing is simple: to coordinate related activities intended to make both the producer and consumer satisfied. . . . Marketing is the performance of business activities that direct the flow of goods and services from the producer to the consumer, to satisfy the needs and desires of the consumer and the goals and objectives of the producer.[3]

Barna believes that the basic concept of marketing is not only transferable to the church, but necessary if the church is to make any headway in the 1990s. Unless we package and promote the gospel in a way our

target audience can appreciate, we will be left without an audience.
Church marketing is the performance of both business and ministry
activities that impact the church's target audience with the intention
of ministering to and fulfilling their spiritual, social, emotional, or
physical needs and thereby satisfy the ministry goals of the church.[4]
Barna sees himself as breaking new ground. He contends that seminaries have failed to prepare pastors adequately for doing battle in the
marketplace. "The major problem plaguing the Church," he contends,
"is its failure to embrace a marketing orientation in what has become
a market-driven environment."[5] In the last few decades seminaries
have added counseling and youth-ministry departments; if Barna has
his way seminaries will also be offering classes, maybe even majors,
in how to market the church.

The average pastor has been trained in religious matters. Yet, upon
assuming church leadership, he is asked to run a business! Granted,
that business is a not-for-profit organization, but it is still a business. The Church is in the business of ministry: searching out
people who need the gift of acceptance, forgiveness, and eternal life
that is available in knowing Jesus Christ. For the local church to
be a successful business, it must impact a growing share of its
market area.[6]

In Barna's 1988 book *Marketing the Church: What They Never
Taught You About Church Growth,* he describes the skeptical reaction of many pastors: "Anyone who speaks openly about marketing
any facet of Christianity is likely to be branded 'radical,' if not down-
right 'heretical.' "[7] Evidently Barna has won over a lot of skeptics,
because since he wrote those words marketing the church has become
all the rage. It is standard fare at church-growth seminars, and church
leadership teams all across America are devouring Barna's books.

One of the reasons Barna has been so successful is that he lays out
in practical, concrete terms what a church should do to be effective

in the 1990s. He does not suggest traditional appeals, such as calling for deeper spirituality or developing the spiritual disciplines or praying for spiritual renewal. Let me be clear: he doesn't deny these dimensions; if anything, he assumes them. He takes for granted that Christians know the biblical Jesus. The big issue for Barna is how to get other people to know the changeless Christ and buy into the Christian lifestyle.

Seminaries are great for illuminating the doctrines of the faith, says Barna, but deficient in teaching pastors how to project a positive, appealing image. Instead of learning how to reach a target audience in their communities "as cost effectively and meaningfully as might be done by McDonald's, Proctor and Gamble, or American Airlines," seminary students are conjugating Greek verbs and debating sixteenth-century theological controversies.[8]

Marketing, claims Barna, is not about a new way of perceiving the Lord Jesus Christ; it's about coping with change, competing against the world's attractive alternatives and making the gospel responsive to today's consumer. Molding a new customized ministry involves taking the essentials of the ancient faith and contextualizing them for the American consumer. Barna offers nothing that might be perceived as abstract or theoretical. He simply wants the best of business in marketing and management to shape the future of the church. This is where the seminaries have been deficient, he contends, but thanks to his growing popularity, the business of marketing the church is catching on. Seminaries appear to be making a quick about-face and following this latest trend.

### No-Fault Reasons
Many of those advocating a church-growth marketing strategy are doing so for good reasons.

1. They are concerned that a large segment of American culture will

go unreached for Christ if steps are not taken to ensure effective evangelism. They are tired of low-energy, repetitive, irrelevant, preachy presentations of the gospel. They want the Christian faith to be promoted in a relevant, practical, exciting and relational manner. Christianity is not a stodgy, archaic, tradition-bound religion but a fresh, meaningful, life-changing faith.

Church-growth advocates want the old-time religion of their parents—which is remembered mostly for its doctrinal squabbles, boring services and legalistic morality—transformed into a dynamic, entertaining, life-fulfilling experience. Doug Murren, pastor of Eastside Foursquare Church in Kirkland, Washington, explains: "American Christianity is dominated by our parents' generation. And we boomers, despite our desire to return to a real spiritual experience, are unable to relate to a church culture dominated by our parents."[9]

Marketing provides the necessary paradigm shift for moving away from the worn-out forms of the traditional church to the seeker-sensitive, exciting church of the 1990s. One reason church marketing may be gaining greater acceptance is that it appears to be the only alternative to a church stuck in the past, resistant to change and ineffective in proclaiming and living the gospel. Speaking for the boomer generation, Murren writes, "We are fearful as we go back to church that we'll encounter the same irrelevant, distasteful experiences we remember from our youth: dank basements of Sunday School rooms with concrete walls, cheerless music and an environment that promises relationships, but leaves everyone with nothing more than an indifferent handshake after the service."[10]

2. Market-driven churches accept rather than resist the obvious fact that we are a consumer-oriented culture. We are a nation of consumers. If we are going to "contextualize" the gospel for Americans, we'd better make it relevant to consumers.

We are immersed in a highly competitive, materialistic marketplace that vies for our attention from every conceivable angle. If the church is going to be heard, it will have to learn how to compete in the real world. For a culture as consumer-oriented as ours, looking to the marketplace for the ways and means to compete effectively makes great sense.

3. Marketing is a value-free, morally neutral tool that when used properly can lead to better decisions by church leaders and greater productivity. Marketing offers predictable, positive results. It is pragmatic, cost-effective and efficient. It's something we can "do" that produces results.

Surveys, polls, market analysis and expert consultants produce hard data and usable information. Research that fits the computer age. Statistics that lead to strategies, and systems that produce results. In the relational age, church growth has become a science. Marketing offers an appealing sense of sophistication and objectivity. We are attracted to an unsentimental, businesslike approach. Given the right planning and strategizing, effectiveness can be arranged. "If we refrain from getting caught up in the numbers game," says Barna, "and keep our focus on the purpose of ministry, we will find church marketing to be a satisfying challenge."[11] Yet in *User Friendly Churches* Barna uses a ten per cent annual growth rate as one of two bench marks for success.

4. Today's emphasis on marketing the local church follows naturally the tactics employed by many parachurch ministries for nearly forty years. Marketing the gospel to an increasingly consumer-oriented culture has characterized the efforts of crusade and campus evangelistic organizations, televangelism and youth ministries. Christian organizations, working on the cutting edge of the church, have long been sensitive to a marketing environment, consumer orientation and competition for support dollars. Opinion polls, public relations, telemarketing and direct mailing have all been tools of the trade.

Now, many believe, the time is ripe for marketing strategies to be taken up by the local church. Numbers, promotion, public relations, felt-need orientation, technological savvy and organizational excellence have found their way into the mindset of the local church. An image-conscious consumer culture is having a dramatic effect on how we approach preaching, worship, evangelism, church membership and the whole phenomenon of being the church. What was new and innovative to parachurch ministries after World War II is now being applied to the local church.

5. Marketing keeps separate two distinct yet complementary agendas. Now there is an approach to church growth that clearly distinguishes between strategies that produce numerical growth and strategies that produce spiritual growth.

Barna explains that a "holistic view of ministry" involves two sets of tactics: one to grow numerically and another to grow spiritually. He argues that combining a biblical approach to spiritual growth and a marketing approach to church growth is not only practical but also necessary. We only confuse the issue when we spiritualize numerical growth.

There are definite procedures to follow, such as defining the target audience, analyzing felt needs, designing "user-friendly" facilities, implementing youth programs, improving communication and articulating a long-range vision. All of these are independent of specific recommendations for spiritual growth, such as learning how to study the Bible, spending time in prayer, participating in personal and corporate worship, identifying spiritual gifts and exercising faith in Christ.

According to Barna, "The tactics required to develop strong spiritual character . . . are very different from the tactics required to generate numerical growth. Failure to pursue and achieve balance between those competing but complementary interests leads to an unhealthy church."[12]

6. As we might expect, Barna sees in Jesus the premier example of how to market the church. Jesus the Marketer sanctifies a market-sensitive, market-driven approach to church growth.

Even though Barna does not pretend to offer a thorough study of Jesus' alleged marketing technique, he claims Jesus' support in a general way:

> Jesus Christ was a communications specialist. He communicated His message in diverse ways, and with results that would be a credit to modern advertising and marketing agencies. Notice the Lord's approach: He identified His target audience, determined their need, and delivered His message directly to them. By addressing the crowds on the mountain-sides, or the Jews in the Temple, He promoted His product in the most efficient way possible: by communicating with the "hot prospects."[13]

> Don't underestimate the marketing lessons Jesus taught. He understood His product thoroughly, developed an unparalleled distribution system, advanced a method of promotion that has penetrated every continent, and offered His product at a price that is within the grasp of every consumer (without making the product so accessible that it lost its value).[14]

## Labor of Love

The impact of church marketing is already great, and it's growing. In many evangelical circles its acceptance is not only widespread but also unquestioned. For many sincere Christians, concerned over the future of the church, these reasons listed above commend an innovative, problem-solving solution to church growth in the 1990s. They have thrown their energy and resources into marketing without serious questioning or biblical review.

In the chapters to follow, I want to take a closer look at these reasons and see if marketing the church is as helpful as advertised.

We'll begin by considering the church marketers' critique of the traditional church. This will be followed by looking at the specific marketing tactics used to promote church growth. These include identifying a target audience, meeting felt needs, pursuing executive excellence, promoting excitement and competing for people's time.

My purpose is really a prayer, that our "love may overflow more and more with knowledge and full insight to help [us] to determine what is best, so that in the day of Christ [we] may be pure and blameless" (Phil 1:9-10). This is a positive, constructive challenge that will lead us into a deeper understanding of what it means to belong and serve the household of faith, centered in Jesus Christ.

The issues before us are important, not trivial. They have immediate and long-range personal impact. What are the consequences of relating to people as consumers and striving to meet their felt needs? Is marketing a value-free, morally neutral technique that can serve the church? Did God intend for us to deploy two sets of tactics—two different yet complementary strategies—one designed for numerical growth and the other for spiritual growth? These are practical theological issues that are forced upon us by our own time and place. They cannot be avoided.

The questions are clear and deserve an answer. Does marketing enable the church to distinguish between popular opinion and Spirit-led confession? Does it help the church to hold and wield the keys of the kingdom? Does it lead the body of Christ in the joyful yet costly commitment of cross-bearing? Is Christ building his church through marketing?

# 3

# THE
# TRADITIONAL
# CHURCH

There must be no idealization of the church.
And lamentation ought to be restrained.
EUGENE PETERSON

# Dan and Kathy Maxwell are in
their late thirties. They have three small children and live in an upscale
middle-class neighborhood. They really want to be involved in a dynamic, exciting church.

For Dan and Kathy, nothing is more important than their kids.
They dress their kids in the best and make sure their sons are in soccer
and their daughter in ballet. They're always doing fun things; ball
games, parties, vacation trips to Disney World, a week at the beach.
To say the least, life is fast-paced. Making family life a priority means
that several nights a week, Dan ends up working on business after the
kids go to bed.

Several years ago, dissatisfied with the preaching and worship, the

Maxwells left the mainline denominational church they had grown up in. To use their words, they weren't "getting anything out of it." They didn't quite know what they wanted in a church, but they knew they were wasting time where they were. In spite of pressure from parents to remain in the church of their youth, they made the break.

A few of their friends were going to a traditional evangelical church. It had a reputation for Bible preaching and evangelism, which sounded good to Kathy and Dan. Local members of mainline churches criticized the evangelicals for being self-righteous and "holier-than-thou," but the Maxwells decided to check it out anyway.

Their first reaction to the preaching was very positive. They actually had to open their Bibles and follow along as the preacher expounded the passage. People were warm and friendly. The Maxwells were encouraged to attend Sunday school. They seemed to be surrounded by people who really wanted to be in church.

In the weeks that followed, Dan and Kathy received a lot of attention from church people. The Maxwells are positive, energetic people and were immediately pegged as potential "workers." Dan's demeanor exuded success. His warm, affable manner made him very approachable. He took the initiative in greeting people and made them feel important. His cellular phone, luxury sedan and Polo suits pointed to his business success, but he wasn't a proud man. He was more interested in being friendly than showing off.

In no time at all, Kathy and Dan were deeply involved in the church. Dan was asked to lead a men's Bible study-support group, while Kathy became a leader in women's ministry and took her turn in the nursery. The church board consulted Dan on financial matters and involved Kathy in planning social get-togethers. After a year, they were so connected with the life of the church that a newcomer would have thought they had always attended.

It was then that the euphoria of finding a new church home and being accepted by the people began wearing off. The messages that had first impressed them because they were Bible-based began to bore them. They were having trouble connecting their pastor's biblical exposition with their lifestyle. Instead of leaving the sanctuary feeling uplifted and affirmed, they left feeling down and confused. They wanted a lighter, more refreshing message. The pastor tended to be too serious and pensive. Dan and Kathy's old problem of getting little or nothing out of Sunday-morning messages had returned.

In addition, they were more and more aware of friction in the church. Below the surface of this warm and friendly congregation were some deep-seated conflicts, especially on how money was to be spent. Dan and Kathy had been warned that congregational meetings could get pretty rough, but they were unprepared for the harsh words and open hostility vented over relatively insignificant issues. They couldn't believe Christians could act like that and still worship together on Sunday morning.

Added to their discouragement was the growing pressure to be involved at church several nights a week. What had begun as a positive, enjoyable association was becoming a draining duty. Dan and Kathy had trouble saying no without feeling guilty. They resented that people kept asking them to do things without considering how much they were already doing.

With the pressure building, Dan and Kathy began looking for another church. River Oaks Community Church, the fastest-growing church in their area, had just completed a new sanctuary and was already packed out. Everyone spoke so highly of the pastor that they decided to check it out.

Right from the beginning they were impressed. So much was happening at River Oaks that the church needed parking attendants to direct traffic. The pastor didn't seem like a pastor; he was more like a successful businessman. His personality was a lot like Dan's. He was positive, dynamic, a real people-person; he seemed to have the talent for connecting with people. The services moved along at a comfortable pace, with a pleasant blend of humor and insight. The atmosphere was exciting, and the audience responded with enthusiasm.

Dan and Kathy were impressed with the programs for their kids. Everything seemed to run so smoothly, with no hassles and pressure for them to get to work. They could come to church at any one of the optional service times, put their kids in great programs and leave without being pressured to help out. They didn't have that feeling of being tied down and depended upon. They had finally found a church home they could be ministered to without feeling burdened. There were so many support groups in the church that it seemed as if every conceivable need was covered.

The Maxwells felt freer and happier at River Oaks. Decision making was streamlined and didn't cause the friction that it had in the more traditional church. They could enjoy a service, shuttle their kids to great activities and contribute financial support to a well-run operation. They could even skip an occasional Sunday without feeling guilty—something they'd never been able to do in the traditional church.

## Taking the Traditional Church to Task

Marketer George Barna and successful market-oriented pastors such as Doug Murren, Bill Hybels and Leith Anderson offer an insightful challenge to the traditional church. Their critique may be the most important and constructive element in their analysis of the American church. They paint a picture of the traditional church that Christians cannot afford to ignore. Their analysis is sweeping and their judgment clear. According to these marketers and church-growth consultants, the traditional church is better defined by its weaknesses than by its strengths. In short, the traditional church is insensitive, unintelligible, impractical, inflexible and ingrown.

Doug Murren's critique stems from his very first visit to a church when he was eighteen years old.

I found it horrifying! Then I had a dynamic encounter with Christ. But even then, understanding this church stuff was rugged. These church people took so many things for granted that didn't make the slightest bit of sense to me. My first offering experience shook me up, because I didn't know how much to give. And the collection bags looked really odd to me. In addition, I could sing hardly any of the songs because I didn't know them. Yet everyone else—except for a couple of other social outcasts like me—knew. Because my first introduction to the church world was so traumatic, I have determined to make it easier for other people like me to return to and enjoy church life.[1]

Consequently, Murren determined to make everything so simple and understandable to the "first time visitor and utterly unchurched" that they could fully participate in the worship services.[2]

The traditional church, writes Barna, is "losing the battle to effectively bring Jesus Christ into the lives of the unsaved population. . . . Sermons address topics that are not pertinent to people's lives. Programs provide training that will not be used. Facilities lie vacant because we are not aware of opportunities for reaching the community."[3]

## Maintenance Mode

The number-one problem for the traditional church is that it has lost its vision for growth and outreach. "Too often," Barna contends, "the Church hides behind a spiritual facade that is designed to mask our ignorance, fear, or laziness related to the challenges at hand. . . . I am convinced that God equipped us for a purpose, and that the purpose is to expand the Church."[4]

The traditional church is content with a small congregation. "The average Protestant congregation in this country has fifty to sixty adults who regularly attend Sunday-morning worship services. Generally speaking, that is not enough people for a church to prosper—emotionally, financially or, in many cases, spiritually."[5] The traditional church may have a vision for ministry, contends Barna, but it does not have a vision for marketing itself.

The traditional church throws up roadblocks to newcomers, insisting that visitors appreciate an irrelevant liturgy and the idiosyncrasies of an overgrown blended religious family. If you have ever been brave enough to visit "cold turkey" a congregation of under one hundred, you know the awkwardness that your presence creates the moment you walk through the door. Some people are trying to make a good impression, while others are wondering why this stranger has come. They usually assume that you've just moved into the community; why else would you be visiting their church?

During vacations, my family and I have often visited small and medium-sized churches. There have been times when we were greeted with stares and stiff handshakes. I've felt like telling some concerned ushers, "Look, I'm not a spy or a university professor, just an ordinary Christian looking for a household of faith to worship in this weekend."

Sitting in the pew, I have wondered, What if I were really searching for answers and didn't know Christ? What if my life were falling apart? How would the corny announcements, pitiful music and repetitive sermon answer my need? Would there be anyone who would listen to me and be able to offer spiritual direction? What if I were spiritually and morally confused or suffering from a marital breakup; what if my kids were on drugs? I'm afraid I would leave that church feeling that these people didn't care, not just about me but about God, about integrity, about thinking, about each other. I'd walk out of that lethargic, passive congregation not only bored stiff, but convinced that

Christianity's day was past.

Today's church-growth marketers are not interested in excusing such a church. They would prefer to put it out of its misery by competing against it with such a high-energy, relevant alternative that it would die a natural death.

My father-in-law, Paul Long, who was involved for years in church planting in Brazil, would occasionally come upon a church in such a sorry spiritual and moral state that he would announce a church funeral service. On a given date, he would preach a funeral message for the church, declaring the old church with all of its corruption, gossip and adulteries dead! He believed that the only way to resurrect a new work was to bury the old.

### Playing Church

While the market-driven church advertises a freshness that needs no preservatives, the traditional church is stale and out of date. The traditional church has a habit of mind that excuses mediocrity because it is a volunteer organization that is trying to please all sides of the constituency (congregation) as inexpensively as possible.

When church marketers describe the traditional church, they do not have in mind a beautiful, white-steepled colonial church set in a New England village amid wooded hillsides. They envision a suburban church built without style or vision, a facility that is good for little more than Sunday services and Sunday-school classes. The building is often poorly maintained, with repairs and renovations done by amateur painters and carpenters.

Church leaders spend hours in committee debating the color and price of new carpet in the sanctuary or what contractor to use for repaving the parking lot. I have been on church boards that felt persecuted by fire marshals who required the church to meet fire-code regulations. I've known trustees who thought building inspectors were their enemies.

Office equipment and furniture tends to be secondhand and second-rate. Church members who have expensive homes and pay top dollar to have their own lawns and homes maintained professionally begrudge paying a custodian or a lawn-care company to keep up the church building and grounds.

That stinginess carries over into other areas such as staff salaries. In many churches, the people who control the money are in their sixties or retired. They lived through the Depression, and they can't understand today's salaries. Financial management is often delegated to or controlled by individuals perceived as less spiritual than those who are heading up "people ministries." And they often are. People who would never be asked to offer spiritual direction and encouragement to individuals in financial trouble assume ownership of the church's financial matters. Financial and facility management in the traditional church often falls to men who are so task-oriented and reticent to speak of their faith that there is little else they can do. Putting these unspiritual men to work becomes necessary to gain their political support.

I've known churches that divide spiritual and material responsibilities between two boards. The elders, who characteristically are more relational and expressive of their faith, deal with spiritual matters; the directors, who control the budget, deal with the building and bills. The predictable result of this leadership arrangement is conflict between the two boards, because the directors are out of touch with the ministry concerns and initiatives of the elders. What may look like a system of checks and balances in a church's constitution does not take into account the practical politics and dual standards for office in the traditional church.

Running the church reminds me of my high-school experience of "Junior Achievement." This was an extracurricular program designed to acquaint students with business practices in the real world. We were to set up a make-believe company, determine how we were going to manufacture and market a product and then implement our plan.

I suppose it was an educational experience, but it felt quite artificial to me. The program acquainted us with business terminology, but the way we approached business was contrived. It was as if we were pretending to run something that wasn't really there to run.

I can't tell you how many times that Junior Achievement artificiality has come to my mind during church board meetings. Ministry has often been the furthest thing from the agenda as we have worried about what so-and-so would think or debated the process of decision making.

People with little influence in any other sphere tend to use the church as a platform to exert their opinions and project their egos, while others transfer their authority in the professional world into the church. More people have burned out in the traditional church because of church politics than for any other single reason. Lines of authority are muddled, dominant personalities wield power, decisions are controlled more by church bylaws than by biblical principles, and spirituality tends to be either neglected or used to avoid tough decisions and conflict resolution.

People become discouraged about working through the system to get things done. What Tom Wolfe said of city bureaucracies is also true of church boards: "The ability of groups to stop things is greater than the power of anybody to get something done."6 One intellectually sharp and spiritually gifted woman wrote to me recently, expressing her frustration with serving on her church's board of directors and pastoral search committee:

It seems like so many of the older people in our church want the younger people around for their energy and the work they do, but they don't want to give any of us credit for being thinking human beings. I get tired of being patronized and condescended to by individuals who are minimally involved and spiritually uncommitted to the ministries of the church, but who think they know it all!

Old habits certainly die hard, especially when some (many) people don't ever want to change the way they think! It's been a tough couple of months. . . . I'm struggling with what seems to be a conflict between how I really enjoy ministering and what I feel like I have to do. I understand that it's important to have differing perspectives on the search committee and board of directors (especially since many of them understand a church of ten years ago), but it's such an uphill climb. I am constantly a dissenter and I don't enjoy it at all. Unfortunately, the time spent doing those things leaves little time and energy for growth groups and all the other things I so enjoy doing in the church! I'm having a hard time figuring out what's "right" to do despite how I may be feeling. On top of all that I can't stop feeling burned out long enough to get halfway excited about any potential candidates.

Karen is certainly not alone in how she feels. She is called to serve, but her service is frustrated by a group of people who are fearful of losing control and suspicious of the next generation of leaders. Most of the men on the committees she serves have never had to deal with bright, articulate women who are knowledgeable of the Bible and well aware of the world's strategies. With a Ph.D. in educational administration and a keen sense of Christian body life, Karen is hardly about to rubberstamp policies and decisions that make it seem as if we are playing church rather than being the church.

### Paradigm Paralysis

The mentality of the traditional church is generally pessimistic. People spend a lot of time dwelling on the past, rehashing old differences and taking comfort from set styles. They feel burned out, defensive, threatened by change and tired of trying. There is a lack of innovation, options, variety and experimentation. "We've always done it this way" is a discouraging refrain chanted to a generation eager to rethink old forms and reach out to new people.

One year a missions committee decided to drop the children's flag ceremony from the opening meeting of the missions conference because it had been poorly executed the year before. The children had been nervous and awkward, the adult organizers hassled and uptight. Nobody on the missions committee knew why the ceremony had to be done every year. It seemed more like a cute distraction than an appropriate beginning to the conference, so they decided to forgo it.

Parents and children were happy about the decision, but not some of the older members. They let it be known that the absence of the children parading to the front of the sanctuary and announcing each missionary's name and country was the down-side of the whole conference.

Little issues like this make life difficult for anyone assuming responsibility in the traditional church. But if change in such small matters is difficult, consider the friction generated when major changes are proposed. In the corporate world men and women in their thirties are assuming significant responsibilities, but that is not happening in the traditional church. Age and gender are still grounds for disqualification.

Doug Murren argues that any church that is perceived by non-Christians as "a male dominated club" will be judged as spiritually unauthentic. "Where women are not recognized in leadership positions, those congregations will be judged to be morally invalid in the hearts of some and at least a little out-of-touch in the hearts of others."[7]

The same holds true when it comes to singles. Murren contends that the traditional church has a bias against singles.

For far too long, singles have been relegated to special meetings somewhere in the basements of churches. And, for just as long,

singles have been unfairly and unkindly treated as a kind of oddi-
ty—persons that others have to tolerate and deal with until they
finally get married. This attitude is the result of a basic disposition
in the Church that if you're not married, you're either out of the
will of God or your true love is still on the way to rescue you.[8]
It is for these reasons that Barna and Murren believe that the traditional church suffers from paradigm paralysis. Models of leadership,
decision making, outreach and worship follow worn-out forms that
either distort the gospel or distract people who would potentially be
interested in the gospel.

Joel Harper offers an interesting illustration of paradigm paralysis.
The watchmaking market was dominated by the Swiss for years. In
the past, if you wanted a good watch you bought a Swiss watch.
Recognized around the world for their superior craftsmanship, the
Swiss had a corner on the market.

The invention and application of quartz technology changed all of
that. The finely engineered gears and springs were replaced by more
reliable, longer-lasting quartz technology. Gone, too, were thousands
of Swiss jobs. Skilled craftspeople who had dedicated their working
lives to making excellent watches were now out of work.

The striking fact, however, is that neither the Japanese nor the
Americans invented quartz technology. The Swiss actually did, in one
of their own research laboratories. But when the inventors sat down
with company executives, steeped in the long tradition of watchmaking, they met with something less than an enthusiastic reaction. In fact,
the executives were so unimpressed that they didn't even bother to
patent the technology.

At a trade convention in 1968, the Swiss inventors innocently displayed their potentially revolutionary yet greatly undervalued technology. A representative from an American company walked by, and the
rest is history.

Leaders of the Swiss watchmaking industry believed that their success in the past determined their success in the future. They became victims of that success and blinded to new technologies that would revolutionize watchmaking. Having become firmly attached to their traditional method of making watches, they were paralyzed by their own paradigms and had only themselves to blame when the market for their products dried up.

Church-growth consultants will tell you that paradigm paralysis can be seen just about wherever you look in the traditional church. It is evident in the preaching. Sermons are pedantic, doctrinaire, boring, repetitive and predictable. Preachers are insensitive when it comes to using religious jargon. They are uncreative in finding meaningful starting points to connect with listeners. There is too much emphasis on rote learning and not enough material related to life. It is questionable whether Christians advance beyond the ABC's of the faith. Instead of growing in the grace and knowledge of the Lord Jesus Christ, people in the traditional church are often discouraged from asking searching questions and content with pat answers. Adult education in a Christian worldview may not even be a priority. Sunday school is often poorly taught by stalwarts of the church who have a lock on their classes.

Difficult moral and ethical issues are often ignored or treated superficially. Divorce is handled without giving consideration to biblical conditions. Personal opinion and biblical conviction are indistinguishable. Gossip and greed go unchallenged; pharisaical self-righteousness is undetected. Apologetics mechanically matches solutions with problems the way a recorded telephone message relays informa tion.

The strength of church marketing's criticism of the traditional church lies in the fact that so many believers have experienced these stultifying dynamics firsthand. Stymied by arrested momentum, tired of playing church and frozen in old forms, they personally feel the sorry state of the traditional church.

## Is the Critique Fair?

It's not unusual to be critical of the church, nor is it difficult to find glaring weaknesses. Eugene Peterson reminds us:

> Much anger towards the church and most disappointments in the church are because of failed expectations. We expect a disciplined army of committed men and women who courageously lay siege to the worldly powers; instead we find some people who are more concerned with getting rid of the crabgrass in their lawns. We expect a community of saints who are mature in the virtues of love and mercy, and find ourselves working on a church supper where there is more gossip than there are casseroles. We expect to meet minds that are informed and shaped by the great truths and rhythms of scripture, and find persons whose intellectual energy is barely sufficient to get them from the comics to the sports page.[9]

Many people, like myself, have come to Christ and grown up in the traditional church. We have felt the frustration described above. Sometimes the gap between what the church should be and what it is seems overwhelming. We think about dropping out of the church altogether and withdrawing into private spirituality. We contemplate following Christ and divorcing the church, or at least distancing ourselves from it. We attend services, but we don't want to get involved in church politics or ministry pressures.

However common this reaction may be, spiritual maturity offers a different course of action. Spiritual discernment helps us to see that the church is much more than a troubled human institution. The church is the body of Christ, a community of sinners brought together by the love of Christ. "Our membership in the church is a corollary of our faith in Christ. We can no more be a Christian and have nothing to do with the church than we can be a person and not be in a family. ... It is part of the fabric of redemption."[10]

Christians continue to struggle with the natural self and their sin nature. It should not surprise us that our churches, like our families, are constantly dealing with evil. Sometimes the church is resisting, other times yielding, to the forces of evil, but it is never above spiritual conflict. The church does not have the luxury of a hermetically sealed, sterile environment. It operates much more as a spiritual M.A.S.H. unit near the front line, offering the gospel of grace in a broken and sin-twisted world.

Without excusing or condemning the church for its hypocrisy, egoism, duplicity and dishonesty, we need to acknowledge that we have contributed our share of sins to the corruption of the church. But thankfully, even greater than this sad fact is the redemptive truth that Christ continues to offer himself through the Word and the Spirit to us, forgiving, redeeming and sanctifying.

At such times it is more important to examine and change our expectations than to change the church, for the church is not what we organize but what God gives, not the people we want to be with but the people God gives us to be with—a community created by the Spirit's affirmation, reformation, and motivation. There must be no idealization of the church. And lamentation ought to be restrained. Eulogy and anguish are alike misplaced. Churches are not little Jerusalems, either old or new.[11]

Ignatius acknowledged that God uses crooked sticks to draw straight lines. The power of the Spirit comes through broken human vessels, not human perfection.

The apostle Paul distinguished between the sins of the flesh that destroyed the witness of the church and Christlike, incarnational weakness that was essential for witness:

God chose what is foolish in the world to shame the wise; God chose what is weak in the world to shame the strong; God chose what is low and despised in the world, things that are not, to reduce to nothing things that are, so that no one might boast in the presence of God. He is the source of your life in Christ Jesus, who became for us wisdom from God, and righteousness and sanctification and redemption, in order that, as it is written, "Let the one who boasts, boast in the Lord." (1 Cor 1:27-31)

We do not want to excuse the traditional church from a true test of its spiritual character, but neither do we want to transform the church into something the world finds impressive, like the Vatican or the Crystal Cathedral. Judging from the apostolic tradition, the church was never meant to compete with IBM or Disney World on the world's terms, but on God's terms. The church that tries to impress the world falls into the temptation of trying to prove its identity by changing stones into bread. It bows before a secular standard and forfeits its true character.

**Tabernacle Religion**

The book of Hebrews is the New Testament's longest-sustained argument against traditional religion. It is addressed to believers who were pressured to diminish the sufficiency and supremacy of Christ by emphasizing the religious forms and legal codes of Judaism. They were tempted to put their trust in obsolete forms and become "semibelievers" in Christ. They were hedging their religious commitment with deeply rooted traditions that were designed to point to Christ but instead became ends in themselves.

The author of Hebrews responds to this heretical challenge, which was both a doctrinal and a practical distortion of authentic Christian living, with a bold, multifaceted reaffirmation of the total redemptive sufficiency of Christ. His corrective to a church stuck in the past, fixating on religious forms, was a serious reminder to fix their eyes on

Jesus, "the pioneer and perfecter of our faith, who for the sake of the joy that was set before him endured the cross, disregarding its shame, and has taken his seat at the right hand of the throne of God" (Heb 12:2).

Hebrews corrects the problem of the traditional church with a strong theological appeal to refocus life in Jesus Christ. The author calls for a spiritual renewal of the household of faith through an exclusive, persevering commitment to Christ.

Compare this to church-growth marketers' solution for the traditional church. They do not criticize the church so much for its spiritual weakness as for its market insensitivity. They attribute the problems of the traditional church to a generation frozen in time, not to dead orthodoxy. They call for a change in leadership, not for spiritual renewal. "American Christianity is dominated by our parents' generation," laments Murren. "And we boomers, despite our desire to return to a real spiritual experience, are unable to relate to a church culture dominated by our parents."[12]

Paradigm paralysis, church marketers claim, is a generational weakness. The fatal flaw in the traditional church is an older generation's insensitivity to the market rather than a fundamental spiritual weakness. And the solution to this malaise requires a paradigm shift from the maintenance mode to the marketing mode. Their prescription for a church stuck in the past and muddling through the present is not spiritual renewal involving forgiveness, prayer and a deeper insight into the Word of God, but a practical sociological transformation. People who are serious about reaching the thirtysomething generation need to switch their Christendom model of traditional religion for a market-sensitive, consumer-oriented approach that can compete effectively in the post-Christian, secular era.

When marketers quote the proverb "Where there is no vision the people perish," they have in mind a marketing vision, not a ministry vision. They redefine the original intent of the proverb—"Where there is no prophecy [revelation], the people cast off restraint, but happy are those who keep the law" (Prov 29:18)—in favor of a marketing vision for consumer sensitivity, meeting felt needs, excitement and excellence.

No wonder Barna believes it's easier to create a "user-friendly" church from scratch than to work with an old church. "The fact is that it *is* substantially easier to start fresh than to recast an existing body into a new entity."[13] From a marketing standpoint this makes perfect sense. If you are going to start a new franchise with radically different perspectives and innovative techniques, why bother with the headaches of an old company?

The problem is that existing churches are more like old families than old stores. If every generation deserves an innovative contextualization of the gospel, if every target audience has to be appealed to in unique ways, then should the church start from scratch with each new generation and subculture? Would the church be better off without heritage and tradition? But in that case, wouldn't the church also lack wisdom, depth and staying power?

The "starting fresh" strategy of church growth is geared for the consumer who is always shopping for the new improved version of soap. The American propensity for what is new and exciting is so great that our churches will either have to learn to surf the crest of the latest trend or be washed up on shore. Increasing numbers of Christians are already shopping from week to week for the "best buy"—the most exciting worship, the most entertaining pastor and the most convenient parking.

Suppose we succeeded in custom-designing a user-friendly church that had all the "right stuff." Would we have achieved what God desires? Let's say there's plenty of convenient parking. Greeters are warm and informative. Facilities are attractive, functional and maintained with professional excellence. Services are relationally warm, inspiring, easy to follow and exciting. Messages are relevant, uplifting and contemporary in flavor. They meet people where they are, mixing serious content with humor. The pastor is an excellent communicator, quick-witted, engaging and transparent—a cross between an entertaining celebrity and a skilled, experienced CEO. The Christian education program is extensive and well staffed, ministry is geared to each age group and emphasis is placed on fellowship and relationships. There is a large singles group, and support groups come in all shapes and sizes. The atmosphere that pervades the church is upbeat, positive and visionary. There is a real sense that church is going someplace and that ministry can be fun, exciting and rewarding.

Now, suppose that this description fit your church. Would that mean that your church was a true household of faith, a biblical community of Christian disciples? Would it mean that the kingdom of Christ was being served?

Our first reaction may be that any church that has achieved all this must be effective spiritually as well. But a five-star performance rating from church marketers does not necessarily mean that a church is a fellowship of believers, disciplined in prayer, intent on worship and faithful in witness. The marketing achievements listed above can be brought about by setting goals, motivating people, improving public relations and meeting felt needs. A church could master the art of marketing but neglect faithfulness, justice and mercy. The "successful" church may be more entertaining than edifying and more exciting than holy.

The church of Laodicea, described in Revelation 3:14-22, was outwardly impressive but inwardly superficial and weak. They gave themselves high marks for external achievements, but God's internal audit exposed their spiritual apathy and complacency. The church of Laodicea came under God's judgment because they lacked a passion for

God. They were in need of spiritual renewal. There are many ways that a church may appear impressive and exciting, but fail to be faithful to Christ and his kingdom.

# 4

# THE
# TARGET
# AUDIENCE

Generally a pastor can define his appropriate
target audience by determining with whom he would like to
spend a vacation or an afternoon of recreation.

BILL HYBELS

Church marketers believe that
the first step in solving the problem of the traditional church is to
practically determine what segment of the market your church intends
to reach. Lyle Schaller, one of America's most widely read church
consultants, says, "Evangelism in the nineties is niche. You pick out
a segment, a slice of the market you want to try to reach, and develop
a ministry for that slice."[1]

Theoretically there are many groups to choose from, including the
poor, the aged, students, Afro-Americans and Hispanics, but practically, church marketers exclusively target white, middle-class, college-
educated baby boomers, born between 1946 and 1964. Other groups

are rarely mentioned. This is a church-growth strategy intended for children-centered, career-focused, consumer-oriented families that live in the suburbs.

As we said earlier, George Barna distinguishes between two types of tactics, one for spiritual growth and the other for numerical growth. He basically assumes that churches know how to go about developing spiritual growth. There is little question in his mind that evangelicals know the fundamental truths of the gospel. Spiritual renewal and prayer are standard prerequisites that need no explanation; even the traditional church often gets these right. Where the church fails is in establishing its marketability. It needs to position itself positively and creatively to reach those who appear to have the greatest potential for reversing America's moral and spiritual decline. Focusing on this target audience is the church's first tactical move in the battle for America's future.

## The Market Niche

Evangelistic concern for baby boomers is the reason behind the big push for market strategies and consumer sensitivity. Identified by some as the pivotal generation, this numerically significant, financially powerful, high-energy generation longs for community but can't shake nagging feelings of emptiness and disappointment. Baby boomers and their children are the target audience, the market niche, that the innovative, trend-setting churches are shooting for. Analyzing what baby boomers want out of life has become a prerequisite for developing a market strategy. The market profile that emerges guides the market-sensitive church in meeting the needs of a special generation.

The goal of "target marketing," according to Barna, "is to be as specific as possible in selecting the audience to whom you will market the product. By matching the appeal of your product to the interests and needs of specific population segments, you can concentrate on getting your product to your best prospects without wasting resources on people who have no need or interest in your product."[2]

*1. Consummate consumers.* First and foremost, boomers are consumers. "Boomers have always been the prized jewel of marketers."[3] They not only represent the most powerful market share but also have been conditioned through years of prosperity to expect "satisfaction guaranteed, or your money back." Post-Depression, post-World War II Americans have cultivated a "we-expect-more-of-everything" attitude. Their inflated desires are stimulated and fed by a culture that sees satisfaction almost exclusively as a marketable commodity.

The baby boom generation has developed a consumer mentality about virtually everything. This is especially evident in what church marketers are telling us boomers are looking for in church. It takes money to lure baby boomers into church. Today's felt needs begin with a list of consumer expectations that would have made Jesus' ministry impossible.

When Leith Anderson compares the traditional church to today's market-sensitive church, he begins with the popular automobile advertising jingle "This is not your father's Oldsmobile." He does so to set up a contrast and teach a lesson; the church of the nineties cannot afford to be a church of the fifties. "Not that there's anything wrong with a 1954 Olds," says Anderson. "It's just not a car for the 1990s. It had no seat belts, no air conditioning, no cassette deck, no radial tires, no pollution control equipment, and no cruise control. What was state-of-the-art in automotive technology and design forty years ago is now barely acceptable for basic transportation."[4]

Anderson is right when he argues that the church must not be locked into the past. Of course Christians need to contextualize the gospel for the present generation. But his implication is that "the new improved version" of the church, one that is suitable for the nineties, has to have a lot of expensive extras in order to prove its worth to the modern, materialistic religious consumer.

Today's consumer is looking for professional child care, fully staffed Christian education departments, exciting youth programs, a dynamic singles ministry, plenty of parking and convenient service times. The modern American consumer is conditioned to look for the best possible deal for the lowest possible price. Given this pervasive consumer orientation, the critical question is, how materialistic does the church have to become to be spiritually effective? Put conversely, to what degree is the church to be countercultural, bucking consumerism for the sake of the kingdom of God?

Secular prophets, who make no claim to be speaking from a Christian perspective, seem to be more astute on this issue than church-growth consultants. Christopher Lasch, for example, warns against the dehumanizing power of consumerism.

In a simpler time, advertising merely called attention to the product and extolled its advantages. Now it manufactures a product of its own: the consumer, perpetually unsatisfied, restless, anxious, and bored. Advertising serves not so much to advertise products as to promote consumption as a way of life. It "educates" the masses into an unappeasable appetite not only for goods but for new experiences and personal fulfillment. It upholds consumption as the answer to the age-old discontents of loneliness, sickness, weariness, lack of sexual satisfaction; at the same time it creates new forms of content peculiar to the modern age. It plays seductively on the malaise of industrial civilization. Is your job boring and meaningless? Does it leave you with feelings of futility and fatigue? Is your life empty? Consumption promises to fill the aching void.[5]

If Lasch is right, the market-driven church could easily contribute to the problems of modern society by treating people as religious consumers. In the very place where people deserve to be comforted and confronted by the truth that they are made in the image of God, they are appealed to on the basis of the consuming image. Religious retail is more marketable than eternal redemption and kingdom righteousness. The church ends up looking to the marketplace for the method and means of reaching people with the gospel.

It is difficult to understand how a consumer orientation could be compatible with the ministry of Jesus, especially when you think of Jesus' fiery reaction to those who were making worship more convenient by making sacrificial animals available to weary pilgrims in the temple. After driving out the sheep and cattle and overturning the money changers' tables, Jesus shouted, "How dare you turn my Father's house into a market!"

When religious consumerism invades the place of community worship, the household of faith becomes an extension of the marketplace. It is no longer a place of prayer, but a business. Jesus' consuming zeal for the house of God is in prophetic contrast to ancient and modern forms of consumerism.

Today's violation of Jesus' ethic is not sacrificial animals or even books for sale in the narthex, but a mentality that caters to consumers who are looking for religious bargains, inspirational incentives and cheap grace.

*2. Educated for success.* The second outstanding characteristic of the boomer generation is its high level of education. No other American generation has had the educational opportunity that this generation has had. Experiencing firsthand the scientific revolution, the information age and the technological explosion, baby boomers view education as a prerequisite for success. Increasing specialization, sophistication and professionalization make academic credentials mandatory for getting ahead. Today's college students reflect the growing pragmatism initiated and developed by the boomer generation.

Education has bolstered America's faith in technology as a way out of the complex dilemmas facing humanity. Supplied with ample evidence of human ingenuity in computerization, robotics, medical technology, communications, space research and weaponry, boomers look to education for solutions. American universities have been disseminating a practical Tower of Babel philosophy for decades, encouraging an entire culture to place its confidence in computers and technology. The market-driven church is prepared for this technologically sophisticated, worldly-wise, educated consumer. The church's task is to supplement the relational, spiritual deficit in modern education by providing an alternative atmosphere to round out personal experience. People leave the world of hard facts and calculated figures for a spiritual experience of warm feelings and relational fulfillment. For many, integrating the two worlds is neither expected nor desired. Self-fulfillment requires two types of success, the one material and the other spiritual. The baby boomer returns to church because something is missing from work and family life. The quest for career success does not satisfy the persistent longing for transcendence.

The affluent, college-educated baby boomer arrives at church with a distorted impression of his or her own ability to think through the meaning of life. To be open-minded, in the modern sense, reduces convictions to preferences and moral absolutes to puritanical notions. Students are taught to be closed to absolute truth claims. It is fine to pursue truth as long as no one claims to find it. The intellectual and moral convictions upon which American universities were originally founded are now judged arrogant and intolerant. Modern education has substituted technique for truth, separated values from fact, confused insight with information, valued tolerance over moral integrity and pursued success rather than wisdom.

Indoctrinated in this collegiate atmosphere, baby boomers feel comfortable with cultural relativism (everyone is entitled to his or her opinion) and satisfied with spiritual relationalism (inspirational feelings about oneself, others and God).

Pastor Murren writes, "Your basic boomer is interested in the Bible, but you have to get us over the fear of getting lost in Genesis 1 and 2. As we're the most educated generation in history, we aren't lacking in intelligence. Rather, our fear is that we will look stupid."[6]

*3. American dreamers.* Affluence, technology and education have not left baby boomers more confident or sure of themselves. The Woodstock generation is middle-aging, and it still hasn't found what it is looking for. In many ways, this target audience feels directionless. Boomers expect more and have more than any other generation, but they are also the most dissatisfied and restless segment of American culture.

Boomers want what Paul Tournier calls "the order of appearances: power, wealth, knowledge, prestige, and reputation,"[7] plus a new order consisting of "creativity, leisure, autonomy, pleasure, participation, community, adventure, vitality, stimulation, and tender-loving care."[8] They want to pursue their own inner journey through a hierarchy of inner needs to the creation of a custom-built lifestyle.

Today's success ethic virtually imposes the notion that we have a moral duty to self. The old self-denial ethic, which stressed deferred gratification, has been turned on its head. Daniel Yankelovich observes, "Instead of a concern with moral obligations to others pursued at the cost of personal desire, we have the concept of duty to self pursued at the cost of moral obligations to others. Personal desire achieves the status of an ethical norm."[9] "For the immediate future," says Paul Light, "the focus on introspection and privatization of experience will continue."[10]

Murren agrees: "We baby boomers aren't coming to church to become members. We're coming to experience something. Yes, even to get something. What we're hoping for is some kind, human touch. . . . Secretly, I think we thirty something folks believe that the myth of Woodstock is what the Church, in a certain sense, ought to emulate.

Church ought to be celebrative, informal and spontaneous. . . . The theology of Woodstock is the dream of a generation. . . . The Church's failure to appreciate the impact of Woodstock could cause it to miss a wonderful opportunity in communicating the gospel intelligibly to an entire generation."[11]

It is difficult to take Murren seriously when he calls for a theology of Woodstock. The "myth of Woodstock" may represent informality, spontaneity, self-expression and personal freedom, but the reality of Woodstock, expressed succinctly by one rock musician, was "one hundred thousand people stoned out of their heads wanting to get laid." Far from a symbol of personal freedom, Woodstock was a tragic event expressing the emptiness and alienation of a generation.

The "meism" of the 1970s and 1980s may be yielding to what Yankelovich calls an ethic of commitment—a commitment to something larger than oneself. For most boomers, this means focusing on children and health. The lofty idealism of changing the world for the better has been scaled down to more modest dreams. The new sacred order substitutes health for holiness and familial happiness for God. The baby boomer believes that emotional and physical well-being can be controlled, given adequate education and discipline. Safe sex, not moral sex, is the goal of the 1990s. The fear of cancer eclipses the fear of God.

Today's "incredible range of anxieties, from the fat in an ice-cream cone to the depletion of the ozone layer," distracts boomers from issues previous generations thought were crucial.[12] Americans have scaled down their expectation of salvation and concentrated on immediate tangible, material concerns to the point that they've forgotten how to think about guilt and grace, sin and salvation, heaven and hell. They no longer have the categories to handle such subjects. William Dyrness writes,

It is hard for Americans to understand human life in any transcendent perspective, not because they are perverse or less intelligent than other people, but because they do not have vocabulary or terminology to discuss such ends. Americans are simply incapable of understanding how one might go about meeting a transcendent need. Since physical appetites are so immediately evident and so easily satisfied, it is easy to overlook emotional or spiritual appetites that are deeper and harder to satisfy. We are quite simply so busy fixing things (we have after all a lot of things to fix) that we overlook the plain fact that some things cannot be fixed. Some hungers cannot be satisfied by more self-indulgence.[13]

Boomers have managed to build well-insulated comfort zones. Narcissism rescues the culture from nihilism. People are so absorbed in sex, sports, success and self that even despair has trouble penetrating American optimism. What the church has historically called sin and evil is reduced to personal problems of low self-esteem and insecurity.

The rock group U2 expresses the spirit of the age when they proudly sing their contemporary refrain, "I still haven't found what I'm looking for." The generation targeted by the market-driven church doesn't expect to find ultimate answers or central truths. Many would prefer to be distracted from the search for God, rather than directed. "The baby boomers," says Light, "remain the unseen players in a twenty-year political and social version of 'Waiting for Godot.' "[14]

The profile of this target audience shapes the mood and method of the market-driven church, calling for consumer sensitivity, practical, relational teaching and an optimistic belief in the future. A critical question for the market-sensitive church is whether insight into the mind and culture of the baby boomer generation leads to a prophetic penetration of this market niche with the gospel or promotes a culturally compatible affirmation of the culture. Does the gospel of the market-driven church redeem the lost or reinforce trends, deliver from sin or affirm the self, reconcile people to God or appeal to religious consumers?

### The Quintessential Baby Boomer

Of all the people Jesus encountered, the rich young ruler captures best the ethos of the baby boomer. He was healthy, wealthy and powerful. Easily recognized by his appearance and demeanor as a peak performer, the young man impresses us as intelligent, articulate and respectful. There are some obvious cultural differences—for example, running up to Jesus and falling on his knees doesn't seem quite the yuppie thing to do—but on the whole he was the kind of person that is now being targeted by church marketers.

The question he asked Jesus seemed made to order evangelistically: "Good Teacher, what must I do to inherit eternal life?" (Mk 10:17). Most boomers are not asking such obviously religious questions. They are asking, "How can I feel better about myself?" or "How can I make my marriage work?" But the underlying theme is the same for the rich young ruler and the American Adam. Both are seekers, restlessly looking for personal resolution, knowing that they still haven't found what they're looking for.

Jesus' reply seems unnecessarily abrupt. In fact, by today's standards we might question his "seeker sensitivity." He immediately renegotiated the presuppositions of the conversation. He forced a distinction between human opinion and the Word of God. "Why do you call me good? No one is good but God alone."

The answer the rich young ruler was about to receive from Jesus would be more authoritative than he cared to accept. Jesus began with obedience to the Law: "You know the commandments. . . ." To this the young ruler replied, "Teacher, I have kept all these since my youth."

Today's boomer works from a different list of "commandments" or ideals, including tolerance, focus on the family, optimism, personal achievement and ecological sensitivity. But the same spirit imbues the moral achiever and upstanding citizen: "I am already good enough, I just want to be better." The rich young ruler was interested in betterment; Jesus was interested in transformation. The rich young ruler had in mind remodeling his lifestyle, but Jesus had in mind revolutionizing his life.

This ancient baby boomer was open to suggestions, options and theories, but Jesus was definitive: "You lack one thing; go, sell what you own, and give the money to the poor, and you will have treasure in heaven; then come follow me."

This is not advice from a therapist or inspiration from a motivational speaker. This is a command from God. At this, the young man "was shocked and went away grieving, for he had many possessions" (Mk 10:18-22).

It is sad when Jesus is not enough. We are told that Jesus looked at the rich young ruler and loved him. But the love of Jesus was not enough for this man. He wanted it all: health, wealth, self-satisfaction and control. He knew no other way to see himself than the words we use to describe him—a rich young ruler.

The problem was not Jesus' sensitivity or the relevance of the command, "Come, follow me." The young man knew exactly what was being asked of him, but he chose his opinion over confession and the celebrated individual self over commitment.

The important thing for us to see is that Jesus did not accommodate the gospel to this man's expectations. Far from appealing to the consummate consumer, the self-made success and the imperial self, Jesus made it painfully clear that all that had to go.

## Decategorizing

There are plenty of white, middle-class, college-educated baby boomers who need Christ, but the real world cannot be so neatly segmented. According to Paul Light, "there are four baby boomers at or below the poverty line for every yuppie far above it."[15] Discovering your market niche to be the upwardly mobile, success-driven, child-centered baby boomer may not require focusing on a target audience as much as ignoring the church's mission. Limiting outreach to people who understand our sense of humor, live in similar homes, earn a professional income, share the same family concerns and eat in the same restaurants may create a comfort zone for evangelism, but it may also limit our spiritual growth and dependence upon God.

Decategorizing involves removing the market-niche strategy from church growth—not because it has been proved inefficient or unsuccessful, but because fundamental Christian truth discourages it. As the apostle Paul said, "From now on, therefore, we regard no one from a human point of view" (2 Cor 5:16). We cannot subordinate people made in the image of God, people for whom Christ died, to consumer categories.

"Christian thinking is incarnational," writes Harry Blamires.

The Christian mind surveys the human scene under the illumination of the fact that God became man, taking upon himself our nature, and thereby exalting that nature for all time and for eternity. Thus the Christian's conception of the human person is a high one, his sense of the sacredness of human personality being deeply grounded in revealed theological truth. The status of the personal is such, in Christian eyes, that it ought not, for instance, to be subordinated to the mechanical.[16]

What Blamires terms the "mechanical" or "functional" view of human beings is applicable to the *marketing* view of human beings.

The diversity of Jesus' mission and the unity of the Jewish and Gentile ethnic groups in the early church do not seem compatible with marketing the gospel to a special type of consumer. This goes beyond contextualizing the gospel for needy people to accommodating the gospel to culturally induced felt needs and consumer expectations. The marketing approach compromises the gospel not by denying biblical doctrine in any obvious way, but by denying biblical practice.

Church marketers look at the baby boomer the way shopping-mall retailers look at customers. Success depends on giving people what they want. Meeting emotional and spiritual felt needs becomes a commodity that can be experienced, given the right personalities, performance and programs.

Biblical prophets have looked at culture very differently. One could hardly confuse the prophets' penetrating judgment of culture with a marketing report. Instead of looking to the marketplace to understand what appeals to the human heart, the prophets used the Word of God to penetrate prevailing cultural norms and expectations. They resisted the religious powers' accommodating efforts to reassure people that their greedy consumption, entertaining worship and striving for success met with God's approval.

My fear is that we may be guilty of relating to people superficially as the religious leaders did in the day of Jeremiah: "They have treated the wound of my people carelessly, saying, 'Peace, peace,' when there is no peace" (Jer 6:14). It was necessary for Jeremiah to stand at the entrance into the Lord's house and say to the people who had come to worship, who sincerely considered themselves well-respected, "born-again" believers,

Thus says the LORD of hosts, the God of Israel: Amend your ways and your doings, and let me dwell with you in this place. Do not trust in these deceptive words: "This is the temple of the LORD, the temple of the LORD, the temple of the LORD." For if you truly amend your ways and your doings, if you truly act justly one with another, if you do not oppress the alien, the orphan, and the widow, or shed innocent blood in this place, and if you do not go after other gods to your own hurt, then I will dwell with you in this place, in the land that I gave of old to your ancestors for ever and ever. Here you are, trusting in deceptive words to no avail. (Jer 7:3-8)

The church marketer's analysis of culture is so superficial that it is deceptive. If a Christian desires to understand cultural dynamics and where American culture is headed, he or she would be better off reading such books as Daniel Yankelovich's *New Rules: Searching for Self-Fulfillment in a World Turned Upside Down,* Christopher Lasch's *The Culture of Narcissism* and *The Minimal Self,* Allan Bloom's *The Closing of the American Mind,* Neil Postman's *Amusing Ourselves to Death: Public Discourse in the Age of Show Business* and Robert Bellah's *Habits of the Heart.* These works are far more helpful for illuminating the baby boomer than George Barna's analysis or Doug Murren's advice.

In *The Christian Mind,* British writer Harry Blamires offers this assessment:

> Thus prophetic condemnation of salient features of contemporary secularism comes nowadays from secularists themselves whose ground of judgement is a humanistic one. It is clear that where there is no Christian mind to pass judgement upon society, those who care for human dignity and integrity on other grounds than the Christian's will be provoked to rebel against the multifarious tendencies of contemporary civilization to depersonalize men and women. This rebellion must be regarded as a significant feature of the post-Christian world. It is good in itself. That is to say, the protest needs to be made. What is bad is that it should come from outside the Christian tradition.[17]

### Jesus' Target Audience

"It is easier for a camel to go through the eye of a needle than for a baby boomer to enter the kingdom of heaven."

Did Jesus have a target audience? It's virtually impossible for a serious student of the Gospels to picture Jesus using social rapport, income level, age or culture as a criterion for mission. If discovering your market niche is important for marketing, Jesus' niche was the whole world.

It is difficult to imagine Jesus responding favorably to market segmentation, for he refused to categorize people. Jesus was the best example the church has ever had of how to contextualize the gospel; that is to say, he maximized the impact of the gospel on a person's life without compromising the integrity of the gospel. Jesus proved that discerning how best to present the gospel was different from defining a target audience. His evangelistic effectiveness was tied to sensitivity, not segmentation.

It would be tragic if market segmentation amounted to pitching the gospel to an upscale religious consumer and neglecting the needy and the outcast. The Pharisees may have targeted people like themselves, but Jesus focused on the lost. If anything, he seemed especially responsive to the social outcasts: the disabled, the poor, the prostitutes. Jesus targeted people who needed to repent and turn from their wicked ways and receive the love and mercy of God. "Those who are well have no need of a physician, but those who are sick," Jesus said. "I have not come to call the righteous but sinners" (Mk 2:17).

People who recognized their need were especially receptive to Jesus and the gospel. Focusing on this target audience was as revolutionary then as it is today. When Jesus told his stories of the lost sheep, the lost coin and the lost son, he conveyed to people who were desperately empty, lonely and fully aware of their distance from God that there was hope. He communicated to them a sense of importance and value that they had probably never gained from a rabbi.

When I hear of a pastor who defines his target audience as people he would like to spend a vacation with, I fear that the church has exalted personal preference over Christian mission and has confused discernment with discrimination. The proclamation of the gospel and the character of the household of faith challenge the baby boomer market profile. Tailoring the gospel to fit the consumer distorts the gospel, discounts the work of the Holy Spirit and dehumanizes men and women made in the image of God.

Market research may be fine for the marketplace, where everyone is a consumer, but for the church it offers a superficial, reductionistic view of people. If Afro-Americans, Caucasians and Jews were categorized the way church-growth consultants profile baby boomers, it would be judged as racial stereotyping. It's one thing to understand cultural trends and attitudes in order to discover appropriate starting points for penetrating a culture with the gospel. It's quite another thing to mold the gospel to fit the expectations, aspirations and dreams of the American baby boomer.

# 5
# MEETING
# FELT
# NEEDS

Instead of me fitting a religion I found a religion to fit me.
AD FOR THE UNITARIAN UNIVERSALIST CHURCH

Defining the target audience is the first tactical move church marketers make; meeting their felt needs is the second. Most of these felt needs can be identified and understood by any observer of American popular culture. Secular marketing research can be a valuable tool in assessing what people are looking for in a market-sensitive, consumer-oriented church. Most of what people feel they want can be satisfied by a marketing approach. The theory is that in order to meet people's spiritual needs, the church must first meet their felt needs. Church-growth experts suggest using felt needs as a bridge to more serious needs such as reconciliation with God and Christian discipleship.

"Churches and Christian organizations," writes Leith Anderson, "will not effectively reach baby boomers with 1950s methods and programs."

We must relate to boomers in terms of their distinctions and in response to their needs. Most won't just "show-up" at a Sunday church service to hear the Gospel. They will be attracted by modern nursery facilities, excellent pre-schools, and attractive youth programs for their children. They will become open to the message of Jesus Christ during the transition times of their lives, such as divorce, remarriage, the birth of a child, unemployment, or the death of a parent. But that message will probably get to them through a divorce recovery workshop, an unemployment support group, or a workshop on grief rather than through a sermon. The church that ministers to and accepts people where they are will be much more successful in reaching them with the truth and light they so sorely need.[1]

### Market-Driven Felt Needs

The list of attractions that will lure baby boomers to church is easy to compile. They fall into two main categories: relational needs are most important, followed by tangible conveniences.

The baby boomer wants a warm, supportive, informal and positive atmosphere. Anything that distracts from this will be an instant turn-off, while anything that's done to make the atmosphere nonthreatening improves effectiveness. Sermons are short, simple, uplifting and personally inspiring. Topics are carefully selected to stress the personal over the doctrinal and the relational over the abstract. Sin and money are seldom mentioned. Entertaining features like drama, skits and lively music generate enthusiasm and excitement. Boredom is the bane of the market-sensitive church and must be avoided at all costs. Services are high-energy peak performances, with constant attention to audience retention. Leaders of many market-driven churches have decided against televising their services, but their services are television-ready in any case.

Relational needs are also met on a personal and family level. Many nominal Christians, who have been away from church for years, and non-Christians, who have never gone, are coming to church because of personal crises or family concerns. An array of support groups covering the gamut from eating disorders and addictions to divorce and codependency seek to meet these private needs. There is also a strong relational felt need when it comes to children. For whatever reason—parental insecurity, or a growing sense of parental responsibility, or concern over our culture's moral decline—many parents are coming back to church for the sake of their children. As Anderson says, they are looking for modern nursery facilities, excellent preschools, attractive youth programs and recreational activities. They have high expectations: these services should be provided in a professional and excellent fashion, and parents should not be pressured to volunteer their personal involvement.

In addition to these relational helps, baby boomers are looking for special conveniences. In the nineties, a traditional church facility is not enough. Well-designed, aesthetically pleasing, multipurpose facilities that exude a "hi-tech, hi-touch" atmosphere are increasingly popular. State-of-the-art sound systems, audiovisual capability, FAX machines and computers signal the "seeker" that the church is up to date. These elements remind the religious consumer of the shopping mall or corporate office center rather than the somewhat embarrassing church facility of the 1950s. Buildings and grounds are professionally maintained. Parking is convenient, and ushers and greeters leave a positive impression.

Just how important the look and feel of today's church facility are can be illustrated by Anderson's observation: "Ineffective Christian education and declining Sunday school attendance may not be the result of poor teaching or low commitment; they may be caused by something as simple as the color of the Sunday school rooms. In this case, doing some environmental study could have solved the problem." It may be hard to believe that the color on the walls ranks above good teaching in retaining students, but today's felt needs are as impressionistic as they are market-driven.

George Barna predicts that in the 1990s more than twenty per cent of churchgoers will decide which church to go to on a weekly basis. The traditional definition of a church home will become obsolete. "People will no longer have a single church home but multiple church homes. On any given Sunday they will wake up and choose a particular church which they feel will meet the needs they feel most keenly that morning."[2]

Whether the church wants to or not, it will be forced to compete more effectively in meeting people's felt needs. Because of today's time pressures and emotional stresses, religious consumers will become increasingly selective. "We will have to prove to people that it is worth their time," warns Barna. "We will also have to be more quality-conscious. Since people will be considering multiple options for their time—many of them high-quality options from other institutions, activities, and lifestyles—we will have to show them every time out of the box that we are offering them absolute excellence, relevant activities which will meet their needs."[3]

## Supermarket of Desire

No doubt some of the concerns described above are important and need to be considered in developing a church that is both faithful and effective. Great youth programs, caring nurseries, friendly greeters and support groups are good in themselves and reflect practical Christian concern for others, but are they priorities that necessarily meet spiritual needs? How do we keep attractive peripherals from becoming major fundamentals? How does the spiritual vitality of the church in Acts compare with the performance rating and quality control of the market-driven? Are we creating a competitive environment that inflates expectations among religious consumers and discounts commitment?

If we step back and look at American culture, it's easy to conclude that it is materialistic, self-centered and individualistic. These characteristics raise an important question: What kind of felt needs will be stimulated in the age of entertainment?

The average American household is saturated by television and sports. What does the church need to become in order to effectively compete with frantic schedules, work pressure and leisure amusements?

Parenting is always a challenge, but especially when it comes to meeting one's children's felt needs. I am faced with the uncomfortable and unenviable task of discerning between genuine needs and selfish needs. I would love to give my three children everything they ask for, but few people—not even my kids themselves—would judge me a good father if I did that. If eating, sleeping, working and cleaning were left to my young children's discretion, without any parental direction, our home would be a total disaster. If peer pressure, television ads and self-interest were allowed to dictate the need-meeting in our household, in no time we would be spoiled, self-centered and broke.

What my children really need from me is the ability to discern between momentary pleasure and long-term happiness. They need help in disciplining their lives, deferring gratification and deciding what is right. Much of what they want may get in the way of what they need. They need the example of parents who turn to Christ to meet their deep-seated spiritual needs and human aspirations. Ginny and I have the task of weaning them from superficial, self-centered felt needs and preparing them to deal with their own significant needs and the needs of others through Christ and through responsible, mature behavior.

Being a parent involves daily work in this area. We are not just meeting needs; we are working at defining needs. There is a lot of discerning and discarding to be done.

What holds true for children is also true for adults. The needs we feel most keenly may be trivial or artificial, induced by a culture that is seriously devoted to treating us like consumers every minute of the day. Even when our felt needs are concerned with important matters, such as where to live and work, they may still marginalize more fundamental needs, such as the need to know God.

A recent Volvo ad illustrates how Americans look at "serious" felt needs:

I DO. I DON'T.

ONE KID. TWO KIDS.

PUBLIC SCHOOL. PRIVATE SCHOOL.

START YOUR OWN BUSINESS. PLAN YOUR CAREER.

STOCK MARKET. CDs.

BUY A PERFORMANCE CAR. BUY A SAFE CAR.

DESIRE. NEED. PASSION. RESPONSIBILITY.

RESPONSIBILITY. PASSION. NEED. DESIRE.

THE DICHOTOMY OF LIFE STARES US RIGHT

IN THE FACE EVERY DAY.

CHOICES THAT DEFINE HOW WE LIVE OUR LIVES

AND WHAT IS IMPORTANT.

WHERE WE CHOOSE TO LIVE?

WHAT SCHOOLS TO SEND OUR KIDS TO?

A FAMILY VACATION?

ANY VACATION AT ALL?

PROTECT THE ONES YOU LOVE.

TAKE SKYDIVING LESSONS.

CAN ONE BE RESPONSIBLE AND NOT BE BORING?

DREAMS? REALITY?

QUESTIONS WE ALL ASK OURSELVES EVERY DAY.

## CAN A CAR COMPANY POSSIBLY HAVE
## ALL THE ANSWERS?
## NO, BUT WE MAY HAVE ONE.[4]

The Volvo ad articulates well the poetry of consumer choice and subtly establishes the boundaries of felt-need expectation. The choice begins with me. "I do. I don't." It involves family, career, finances, self-esteem and image. The questions identify the baby boomer's range of concerns: where to live, what car to drive, how to have fun. Volvo knows that most baby boomers do not want to choose between safety and performance, responsibility and adventure, desire and need. They want it all.

We have grown accustomed, in our market-driven culture, to yoking relational well-being to material well-being. Like the proverbial monkey whose hand is trapped in the cookie jar because it is unwilling to release its grip on its precious find, Americans are trapped by their materialistic dependencies. Barna predicts,

> We will remain a society struggling with self-doubt and low self-esteem. As technological advances and the deterioration of social skills continue, Americans will feel increasingly isolated. . . . Our dominant obstacle to emotional attachments will be our fear of being hurt and our unwillingness to sacrifice material comforts or leisure experiences in exchange for new relationships. Psychological counseling services will boom in the 90's, as people struggle with issues of self-worth, loneliness and control.[5]

It's not surprising that in a consumer-oriented culture the deep-seated spiritual longing for transcendence is scaled down to a materialistic quest for success. For many Americans, the fear of God is nothing compared to the fear of personal failure. Job security means more than eternal security. People who shrug their shoulders at the thought of divine judgment cringe at the thought of cancer or AIDS.

In the nineties, the human search for meaning and significance is translated into a restless quest for excitement and escape. The greatest danger facing the modern psyche is not nihilism but boredom. Qualities honored in the past—stability, continuity and tradition—are exchanged for sensationalism, stimulation and excitement. Today's hunger and thirst for righteousness are nothing compared to the insatiable appetite for entertaining distractions. The impact of sporting events on Sunday worship is only a small example of this phenomenon. Super Bowl Sunday climaxes an entire NFL season that effectively competes for and wins the passion and zeal of millions of Christians. The NCAA Final Four Basketball Championship can outweigh the impact of Easter in churches located in university towns.

When we lived in Bloomington, Indiana, home to Indiana University, I was conscious of a weekend mentality that invariably diverted energy away from worship and the household of faith. Emotionally, the church came in second to home football games, the Little 500 bicycle race, Sunday-afternoon basketball games, the annual antique show, the hospital's gala Christmas banquet, fraternity and sorority "rushes" and Christmas shopping. People looked for something exciting to happen on the weekend. If they had the time and energy, they fit in a church service.

I came to the conclusion that the secularism of a small Midwestern town can be more potent than that of a large city, because the distractions can be more focused and concentrated and therefore more effective in diverting people from their spiritual needs.

If the quest for success is more important than spirituality and excitement is a greater felt need than significance, it's not surprising that individualism competes against the human longing for community. Self-interest dominates the American felt-need agenda to such an extent that self-fulfillment becomes virtually impossible. Each individual becomes the ultimate source of authority. As Daniel Yankelovich explains, "People unwittingly bring a set of flawed psychological premises to their search for self-fulfillment, in particular the premise that the self is a hierarchy of inner needs, and self-fulfillment an inner journey to discover these. This premise is rarely examined, even though it leads people to defeat their own goals—and to end up isolated and anxious instead of fulfilled."[6]

## Bridge or Barrier?

If the logic of felt needs dominates church-growth strategy, what will become of deep-seated spiritual needs? How will a culture that thrives on a consumer ethos become a church obedient to Jesus' kingdom ethic without a major transformation of values? Can Americans make the transition from the Imperial Self to the Incarnate One by catering to the natural self instead of crucifying it?

In spite of the prevailing perspective of church marketers, felt needs may be a barrier rather than a bridge to meeting spiritual needs. A closer look at the importance of the sermon and the character of fellowship in the market-driven church helps to clarify the issue.

## Seriously Unserious Sermons

"When I preach," Doug Murren explains, "I figure I have about one or two minutes for people to decide if they want to listen to me or not."[7] He compensates for this pressure by selecting his sermon topics from the self-help section in the local bookstore and surveying people in his church for pressing needs. These have included the following:

1. How can I have a happier marriage?
2. How can I handle my money better?
3. I don't like my job. What can I do about it?
4. How do I get guidance about my employment?
5. Will I be caught in an ACOA (adult children of alcoholics) pattern all my life?
6. How did we get the Bible? How do I know it's God's Word?

7. How can I be a better parent?
8. How can I get more time for myself?
9. How can I feel better about myself?[8]

Besides "how-to" sermons with practical "take-away" points, Murren advises pastors, "Limit your preaching to roughly 20 minutes, because boomers don't have too much time to spare. And don't forget to keep your messages light and informal, liberally sprinkling them with humor and personal anecdotes."[9]

Barna compares market-sensitive, felt-needs preaching with Christ's strategy and apostolic preaching. Presumably today's market-driven pastors are doing what Jesus did when he shared the gospel with Nicodemus or the Samaritan woman or the man who haunted the Gerasene hills. Barna does not illustrate the connection between Jesus and today's marketing approach, he merely states it. Upon reflection, however, it is difficult to equate Jesus' encounters recorded in the Gospels and the apostolic preaching found in Acts with today's audience-pleasing, consumer-sensitive sermons. It is stretching the imagination, not to mention the meaning of contextualization, to say they have similar motives and methods.

The fact that Jesus and the apostles were sensitive, creative communicators is undeniable. What divides their preaching from modern preaching is the focus of their sensitivity and the nature of their creativity. Unquestionably, New Testament preaching was personally powerful and culturally relevant. The reason for that was its ability to sweep aside superficial felt needs and penetrate to deep-seated spiritual needs. Biblical preaching was God-centered, sin-exposing, self-convicting and life-challenging—the direct opposite of today's light, informal sermons that Christianize self-help and entertain better than they convict.

There are so many illustrations in today's market-sensitive sermons that the hearer forgets the biblical truth that is being illustrated; so many personal anecdotes that the hearer knows the pastor better than she knows Christ; so many human-interest stories that listening to the sermon is easier than reading the Sunday paper; so practical that there is hardly anything to practice.

No wonder nominal Christians leave church feeling upbeat. Their self-esteem is safely intact. Their minds and hearts have been sparked and soothed with sound-bite theology, Christian maxims and a few practical pointers dealing with self-esteem, kids or work. But the question remains: has the Word of God been effectively and faithfully proclaimed, penetrating comfort zones and the veneer of self-satisfaction with the truth of Jesus Christ?

Neil Postman argues that "television-based epistemology pollutes public communication and its surrounding landscape."[10] Nowhere is this more evident than in preaching. The market-driven church is not especially concerned about expounding the Word of God or teaching the whole counsel of God in a consistent and comprehensive way. Biblical expositional preaching has become an anachronism in American culture. Americans in or outside the church do not listen to someone expound on an idea for thirty minutes; that would require them to be attentive and follow a train of thought. This mode of communication is rarely practiced even in the university.

Preaching, like all forms of instruction, faces increasing pressure to accommodate itself to an audience shaped by television. Postman writes:

Changes in the symbolic environment are like changes in the natural environment; they are both gradual and addictive at first, and then, all at once, a critical mass is achieved, as the physicists say. A river that has slowly been polluted suddenly becomes toxic; most of the fish perish; swimming becomes a danger to health. But even then, the river may look the same and one may still take a boat ride on it. In other words, even when life has been taken from it, the river does not disappear, nor do all of its uses, but its value has been seriously diminished and its degraded condition will have harmful effects throughout the landscape. It is this way with our symbolic environment. We have reached, I believe, a critical mass in that electronic media have decisively and irreversibly changed the character of our symbolic environment.[11]

Ironically, popular preachers in the market-driven church lament their audience's biblical ignorance and joke about biblical illiteracy. Yet they are the ones reacting to cultural pressure by scaling down serious biblical reflection. They would sooner entertain their audiences than risk being criticized for being too serious, abstract and boring. Apparently, evangelical preaching must no longer engage the intellect in order to be effective. It can now bypass the mind and focus directly on feelings. As one pastor said, "A good sermon should make us laugh and cry." He did not say, "A good sermon should make us think and act."

If, as Postman argues, "entertainment is the metaphor for all discourse," we are left without a popular medium through which we can communicate the gospel. How can we bring the message of Jesus to a lost and hurting culture in a light-hearted, entertaining, upbeat way?

I recall the time I was asked to speak to Indiana University's football team the night before a big game. I was told that the players would be so preoccupied about the game that it was best not to tell any jokes. Those who had tried humor in the past were usually confronted with stony silence. When the players filed into the room for "chapel," I was thankful for the forewarning. Without exception, every player was intensely preoccupied about the next day's game. They spoke in hushed tones, and their faces were serious. It would have been hard to imagine a more serious mood even if these young men had been going into battle.

The seriousness and intensity of that pregame chapel reminds me of what this culture takes seriously. Intensity is more culturally accept-able in sports than in spirituality. When it's only a game we can afford to be emotional, but when it concerns eternity we are looking for amusing anecdotes.

If preaching is to fit the culture, it will have to adjust to the expec-tations of popular discourse. This is why so many special speakers in evangelical circles are promoted as funny and entertaining. If, how-ever, preaching resists the culture, as I believe it must if the Word of God is to be proclaimed, it will have to become a countercultural medium. Both the medium and the message will be "gospel."

Overhearing a friend praising a popular preacher as one of the funniest speakers he'd heard in a long time, I was reminded of Post-man's question, "To whom do we complain, and when, and in what tone of voice, when serious discourse dissolves into giggles? What is the antidote to a culture's being drained by laughter?"[12]

### The Fellowship of Excitement
For a word that rarely occurs in the Bible, "excitement" has become a remarkably valued prerequisite for consumer-oriented church growth. It is vitally important that churches be committed to having fun. If the atmosphere is charged with excitement, and if leaders exude enthusiasm, then boomers—longing for an upbeat, uplifting expe-rience—will flock en masse. Everything from worship to preaching is required to be exciting.

I was first introduced to this nineties church-growth concept in Houston, Texas. My first impression of Second Baptist Church was formed when I got off the bus from the airport. I was a delegate to the Congress on Biblical Exposition, visiting one of the largest evan-gelical churches in America to hear what Chuck Swindoll jokingly called "the great American preach-off." When I stepped off the bus I was greeted by a 250-pound uniformed policeman, toting a .359 Magnum. I assumed he was a Houston policeman, until I saw the shoulder emblem that read "Second Baptist Church." Here was a church as I had never seen before. It had its own police force and, as it turned out, just about everything else.

If you ever get bored at Second Baptist, you can lift weights, shoot pool, play basketball, browse in the bookstore, eat lunch in the cafeteria, take in a play or attend a support group. This state-of-the-art megachurch, with its corporate campus and full-service subculture for twelve thousand, epitomizes market-driven excellence and excitement.

Houston's Second Baptist takes pride in its marketing approach. Quoted in *The Wall Street Journal,* David Hatton, who is in charge of parking operations, summed it up: "You know the saying: 'The customer's always right.' We've kind of employed that theme, which I think is excellent, much like a fine hotel or a country club."[13] Apparently the church that calls itself the "Fellowship of Excitement" has few reservations, if any, about marketing the church to the religious consumer and using just about any means to close the deal. Whatever it takes to sell Second Baptist to the unchurched is conceivable: sports teams, rock concerts, entertaining plays, felt-need sermons and even World Federation-style wrestling matches.

Gustav Niebuhr reports,

Last summer, to perk up attendance at Sunday evening services, Second Baptist staged a wrestling match, featuring church employees. To train for the event, 10 game employees got lessons from Tugboat Taylor, a former professional wrestler, in pulling hair, kicking shins and tossing bodies around without doing real harm.

"People think because we're a church, maybe we shouldn't market," says Gary Moore, Second Baptist's music minister. "But any organization, secular or otherwise, if you're going to grow, you've got to get people to buy into the product."[14]

Second Baptist Church may be an extreme case, but the strategy for attracting people through marketing felt-needs satisfaction is gaining in popularity. Besides cultural expectation and consumer demand, the roots of this approach lie in the impact of youth ministry on adult ministry. Those responsible for reaching adults are taking their cue from youth ministries. In fact, many of today's most successful, market-driven senior pastors started out as phenomenally popular youth pastors. They were able to make the transition from young people to adults easily by accentuating felt needs and excitement to lure adults to church.

In the past—the ancient past, that is—young people did not look to the church for amusement. In an effort to transfer the riches of faith to the next generation, senior pastors offered young people catechistic instruction. This education in Christian theology was considered essential for an adult faith. Fundamental Christian truths were learned, and important biblical texts were committed to memory.

Most adults today who grew up in the church remember a different kind of youth ministry. Post-World War II youth ministry concentrated on peer-group segmentation, "entry level" evangelism and having fun. Incentives for participation switched from aspiring for Christian maturity to having a blast with your peer group. No wonder baby boomers reared on fast-food spirituality and youth-group activities expect a similar blend of entertainment and excitement scaled to their thirtysomething tastes. Barna observes, "For churches to consistently garner attendance and involvement at events and programs, there must be greater variety in what is offered. The American public has a low tolerance for repetition."[15]

In order to meet this insatiable hunger for excitement and innovation, the wave of the future may be marketed as "Skydome Spirituality." A friend invited me to see the Toronto Blue Jays play in the Skydome, Toronto's new multimillion-dollar sports facility with health club, hotel, Hard Rock Café and numerous restaurants. With a little imagination, I could envision this state-of-the-art ballpark serving as home field for the First Church of Felt Needs.

The fifty-thousand-seat stadium-sanctuary pulsates with sights and sounds. A television monitor the size of a basketball court provides instant replays, close-ups and constant commercial messages between innings. From time to time the camera highlights an enthusiastic fan or a couple who have just announced their engagement. There is never a dull moment in the Skydome. Eyes drift from the television monitor to the playing field. At one point, at least thirty thousand spectators are riveted to the monitor, watching the pitcher clean his spikes with a spoon. The ball game seems both central and peripheral to the event—almost an excuse for the masses to gather, an escape from having to do something.

In the future, the church will learn how to market itself the way the Skydome does. Event Sundays will pull in thousands. Huge monitors will follow the platform performance and keep our attention. The anonymous crowds will serve as a distraction; sheer numbers will serve to define significance. On the day I visited the Toronto Skydome, I wouldn't have been surprised to find church-marketing scouts taking notes and plotting strategies for Event Sundays when the First Church of Felt Needs would take the field.

A mighty marketing fortress such as Houston's Second Baptist reminds me of Martin Luther's visit to Rome. It was there, at the center of religious power and success, that his spiritual sensitivities were shaken and the passion for reformation provoked. The advantage Luther had over many American Christians was the shock factor. He traveled from his Wittenberg parish to St. Peter's on foot. He was unaware and unsuspecting of the felt-needs approach that characterized the Church of Rome. Luther had had no opportunity to become acclimatized to the rarefied atmosphere of spiritual indulgence. It took him by surprise. Unlike the frog in the kettle—unaware of the danger because the water is heated to a boil gradually—Luther felt the danger immediately, deep within his soul. The church he loved was more than an embarrassment or disappointment; it was his sorrow. Eventually, he would rebel.

### The High Cost of Attraction

True worship, like authentic preaching, is foolishness to the world. "Most Christians feel that absurdity," writes Eugene Peterson.

> Some feel it to the point of abandoning it. . . . There are others who do not desert the place of worship, but in staying do something worse: they subvert it. They turn it into a place of entertainment that will refresh bored and tired consumers and pump some zest into them. . . . The dangerous attendees are those who, restless with the nonaction of worship, subvert it into something that will make something happen.[16]

Church marketers have underestimated the cost of a felt-needs approach in four significant ways. First, the expenditure of emotional energy, material resources and personal commitment to meet the high expectations of affluent baby boomers diverts resources from global missions and social justice concerns. The suburban market-driven church is isolationist. Its primary, if not exclusive, focus is on its designated baby boomer target audience. Other commitments are peripheral to its stated mission purpose.

Second, church marketers are depending upon time-pressured, family-focused, career-centered baby boomers to meet consumer demand. As older members—those who were reared with a traditional sense of duty and a generous spirit of giving time and money—retire from duty, boomers will face the stress and strain of meeting unrealistic, self-centered expectations. Will they be able to handle the financial and managerial responsibilities necessary to create a full-service Christian subculture without burning out and dropping out? Eventually, these leaders may begin asking whether culturally induced felt needs should be driving the church anyway. Who, after all, is lord of the church: the consumer or Christ?

Third, there is a price to be paid for marketing the gospel. Church marketers eagerly accept this price: popularity. In the past, Christians gave up popularity when they accepted the gospel. They became countercultural. But now the gospel is reduced to popularity. Doctrinal affirmations remain the same, and the tenets of the faith go unchallenged, but the church is more like a religious shopping mall than a household of faith.

Evangelicals have historically resisted a naturalistic reduction of biblical truth. In the early twentieth century, evangelicals were critical of the "social gospel" for various reasons, including what they considered to be a naturalistic or liberal interpretation of the Bible. Even though the social gospel was laudable in its concern to apply biblical justice, evangelicals resisted the movement, fearing that the essential truth of the gospel would be lost to modernism.

In the late twentieth century, evangelicals resisted liberation theology because they were concerned that the movement politicized the gospel. Liberationists gave the "epistemological privilege" to the poor (Postman would argue that Americans have given "epistemological privilege" to television). In other words, the locus of truth and authority was not vested in biblical texts or church authorities, but in the people. The "magisterium of the people" decided that truth was found in the struggle against economic oppression and for social justice. Once again, evangelicals for the most part rejected the movement. Even though the biblical cry for justice could be heard in liberation theology, evangelicals were not prepared to reduce Christianity to what appeared to be political and economic salvation.

The evangelical resistance to naturalistic and economic reductionism raises an important question. Why have churches and seminaries that have been critical of the liberal social gospel and political liberation theology been so uncritical of church marketing? Can we afford to reduce the gospel to popularity and privatization any more than we can afford to reduce it to politics and social reform? Is it enough to say that the church is doctrinally pure when its praxis is following the world?

Stanley Hauerwas and William Willimon wisely observe: "The church does not exist to ask what needs doing to keep the world running smoothly and then to motivate our people to go do it. The church is not to be judged by how useful we are as a 'supportive institution' and our clergy as members of a 'helping profession.' The church has its own reason for being, hid within its own mandate and not found in the world."[17]

Fourth, a felt-needs approach holds the church hostage to the tyranny of our desires. Has there ever been a time in American history when we have been more self-focused than today? We are bombarded at every turn by the consuming image, appealing to us to try this and then that to see if we feel better about ourselves.

Instead of catering to self-interest and self-centeredness, the church should be showing people "a road right out of the self."[18] Now is not the time for church marketers to advertise self-discovery. What Chuck Colson says is true: "The church is no longer regarded as a repository of truth, nor a source of moral authority, but merely a place to go for spiritual strokes."[19] In Hauerwas and Willimon's words, "The church becomes one more consumer-oriented organization, existing to encourage individual fulfillment rather than being a crucible to engender individual conversion into the Body."[20]

Church marketing may contribute to the problem of self-obsession rather than solving it. Instead of challenging "toxic faith," marketing may be reinforcing it. Stephen Arterburn and John Felton write,

Poisoned by their constant focus on their own needs, hurts and desire for relief, the self-obsessed have little room left for worshiping God or meeting the needs of others. For people living in this selfish state, it is no wonder that expectations of God are so high. Christ was quoted as telling Peter to show his love by feeding his sheep (i.e., meeting the needs of others). The self-obsessed are not interested in feeding anyone else's sheep or helping others in any way. They concentrate on how others can meet their needs, especially how God can relieve them of their burdens.[21]

The logic of meeting felt needs may not advocate selfishness, but it does a poor job of showing Americans how they can move from self-interest to self-surrender. If felt needs are going to serve as a bridge to meeting spiritual needs, they will have to be transformed from consumer expectations to transcendent aspirations.

No matter how pervasive and dominant the consuming image is in this culture, we know that every person has been made in God's image and longs for the reality of transcendence, significance and community in a way that only Christ can fill. No amount of money or entertainment can satisfy this longing or resolve the sin problem that frustrates it. Whatever approach the church uses to communicate the gospel must be consistent with Jesus' invitation, "If any want to become my followers, let them deny themselves and take up their cross daily and follow me" (Lk 9:23).

# 6
# TRANSFORMING
# FELT
# NEEDS

It is not difficult in such a world to get a person
interested in the message of the gospel; it is terrifically
difficult to sustain the interest.

EUGENE PETERSON

John Stott warns, "Unless we
listen attentively to the voices of secular society, unless we struggle to
understand them, unless we feel with modern men and women in their
frustration, their alienation, their pain and even sometimes, their despair, I think that we shall lack authenticity as the followers of Jesus
of Nazareth."[1] This Christlike authenticity will necessarily involve going beneath the surface of consumer-oriented felt needs to discern the
inner pressures and spiritual perplexities of Americans. It will mean
going beyond easily observable religious tastes and emotional preferences. The really pressing needs that Americans feel, the needs Jesus
came to meet, will have to be faced, even though these are the needs

that are generally ignored or distorted in the marketplace. The church is called to address the tragedy and pathos of the human predicament through ways and means that penetrate broken, empty hearts with the good news of Jesus Christ. If the followers of Jesus are to be effective and faithful communicators of the gospel, they need to be receptor-oriented in a distinctive way. It won't help for the church to confuse the consuming image with the image of God, or to pretend to meet people's serious spiritual needs in a light-hearted, casual fashion. At a time when so many are confused over what they really need and want out of life, the church must renew its confidence that Christ is the answer to the quest for transcendence, significance and community.

Now is not the time to scale down our expectations of salvation to humanistic devices. C. S. Lewis reminds us,

Our Lord finds our desires not too strong, but too weak. We are half-hearted creatures, fooling about with drink and sex and ambition when infinite joy is offered us, like an ignorant child who wants to go on making mud pies in a slum because he cannot imagine what is meant by the offer of a holiday at the sea. We are far too easily pleased.[2]

## The Baby Boomer Wish List

There is an inherent conflict of interest in the expectations and aspirations of baby boomers. They long for personal intimacy and friendship, but cling tenaciously to autonomy and self-interest. They want the experience of meaningful community, but resist whatever restricts their personal freedom and fun. Their desire for independence and anonymity conflicts with their felt need for companionship. They have high expectations of what they deserve, but struggle with feelings of inferiority and low self-esteem. They would love to live more meaningful lives, but they devote large blocks of time and energy to television, spectator sports, eating out, working out and shopping. They honestly want the feeling of making a genuine contribution to others' lives, but they guard their personal comfort zones religiously. They expect the best from institutions such as the church, but feel no personal obligation or institutional loyalty.

Perhaps there has never been a generation with such great material and relational expectations, but so little commitment to anything beyond immediate personal pleasure. Eugene Peterson says, "There is a great market for religious experience in our world; there is little enthusiasm for the patient acquisition of virtue, little inclination to sign up for a long apprenticeship in what earlier generations of Christians called holiness."[3] A generation that sets its heart on immediate gratification guarantees spiritual dissatisfaction. The we-expect-more-of-everything attitude generates a disillusioning tension with the pursuit of a more meaningful life.

Daniel Yankelovich insightfully observes,

You are not the sum of your desires. You do not consist of an aggregate of needs, and your inner growth is not a matter of fulfilling all your potentials. By concentrating day and night on your feelings, potentials, needs, wants, and desires, and by learning to assert them more freely, you do not become a freer, more spontaneous, more creative self; you become a narrower, more self-centered, more isolated one. You do not grow, you shrink.[4]

Fortysomething parents know how to be good consumers, but they feel like poor spiritual directors. They shuttle their kids from school to music lessons to soccer practice to the church youth group, but they are unable to provide their children with a coherent Christian worldview. That is not to say that a coherent Christian worldview is not on their wish list. It's just that they are so busy pursuing market-driven felt needs that they have no passion or patience to deal with spiritual needs.

The baby boomer faces an inner competition between success and meaning, comfort and discipline, autonomy and community, entertainment and reflection, fun and responsibility. The myth of the American dream is that if you go about it in the right way, you can have it all. But the reality is a bewildered, unfocused, fragmented person who is either unable or unwilling to choose between superficial felt needs and deep-seated human aspirations. The responsibility of the household of faith is not to compete for the consumer's attention in the spirit of the marketplace, but to provide a Christ-centered alternative. The pervasive, escalating promotion of novelty, noise, excitement and indulgence requires taming and transforming.

**Need-Meeting Jesus Style**
Jesus' feeding of the five thousand and the discourse that followed provide a significant case study in transforming felt needs. John's description of the event (Jn 6) offers an insight into the types of needs Jesus met and his ability to meet those needs without compromising the gospel. This particular incident challenges the appropriateness of calling Jesus a marketer and gives us a picture of how Jesus would handle communication to a modern audience.

Os Guinness describes the profound changes advertising, television and pop culture have brought in public discourse, "above all in the shift from word to image, action to spectacle, exposition to entertainment, truth to feeling, conviction to sentiment and authoritative utterance to discussion and sharing."[5] The communication dynamics Guinness attributes to modernization also apply, to some degree, to the feeding of the five thousand and Jesus' discourse on the bread of life. Then, as now, the audience was more interested in the medium than the message. The "signs" or miracles attracted attention and caused a sensation, but did not lead to reflection and understanding.

The process of moving from a tangible, physical felt need to a deeper spiritual need was emotionally and spiritually painful for the crowd. In fact, if we were to judge Jesus' communication effectiveness quantitatively, it would add up to failure. He went from more than five thousand eager spectators to twelve intense listeners.

Jesus certainly did not win "The People's Choice Award" that day, nor did his message rank in the Top 40 pop chart. But what he did do was to establish a communication model that helps the church to shift from image to word, spectacle to action, entertainment to exposition, feeling to truth and opinion to authoritative utterance.

Jesus does not offer a lesson in how to make the gospel popular, but he does show us the gospel's power. Each stage in this sequence of action and discourse is instructive in transforming felt needs.

*1. From competition to compassion.* Looking out over the approaching massive crowd, Jesus asked Philip, "Where shall we buy bread for these people to eat?" The question undoubtedly took Philip by surprise, because up to that point feeding the multitude had not been his problem, nor anybody's problem in particular. But the question implied responsibility and obligation. It was as if a huge need was suddenly thrust upon Philip.

Confronted, but probably not convicted, by this overwhelming need, Philip immediately thought in terms of budget. He could hardly be blamed for thinking first of how much money it would take to feed all these people. Nor could he be blamed for thinking how much it would cost to give each person even a bite! The very least the disciples could do would cost too much. We are told by John that Jesus asked this question only to test Philip. Jesus already had in mind what he would do.

Philip was confronted with something even greater than a colossal human need. He was faced with the opportunity of placing his faith in the Messiah to meet that need. Jesus' question was an invitation to go beyond conventional thinking and to look at meeting needs from a radically different perspective.

There are two things we can learn with Philip from this first stage of communication. First, he was challenged with the responsibility of meeting the people's felt need for food. Jesus designated this basic human need as something significant enough to engage his and the disciples' attention and energy. If the people of God truly believe that men and women are physical and spiritual beings, made in the image of God, then there will be genuine concern for their physical and emotional welfare as well as their spiritual wholeness.

The physical and spiritual dimensions of human nature are inseparable. The person must not be compartmentalized. As John Stott says, "Our neighbor is neither a bodyless soul that we should love only his soul, nor a soulless body that we should care for its welfare alone, nor even a body-soul isolated from society. God created man, who is my neighbor, a body-soul-in-community."[6] Jesus acknowledged the validity of meeting this physical need independently of any other consideration.

Second, Philip learned that an important feature of this particular need was its power to connect with humanity's spiritual need. Unlike many of the needs the market-driven church is asked to meet, such as the felt need for amusement and entertainment, the need for food can be a powerful analogy for the even more profound need of spiritual nourishment. Meeting people's physical needs has the potential for being an important bridge to meeting their spiritual needs. Bread, in this case, becomes a redemptive analogy, a visual aid to underscore the importance of spiritual nourishment from the one, true and only source, the Bread of Life.

As we shall see, the value of meeting this physical need and its significance in facilitating awareness of spiritual needs was not based on numbers. The success of this redemptive analogy is its appropriateness to the human person rather than its popular appeal.

Giving people simply what they want may satisfy certain felt needs but make it more difficult to give them what they truly need. Obviously there is a difference between a felt need for food and a felt need for entertainment. Meeting a basic human need is inspired by God and motivated out of compassion. Meeting a culturally induced felt need caters to selfishness and is motivated out of competition.

If a church is providing a music program and youth ministry as a "come-on" to attract people, it is compounding the difficulty of communicating the gospel, but if it is counselling broken families, ministering to the poor in the inner city and educating people in the whole counsel of God, it is empowering the gospel. Two church programs may appear identical on the surface, but the motivation and focus can make the difference between an attractive "lure" and an expression of Christ's love.

The needs that Jesus met never trivialized the gospel. Sadly, this cannot be said of the American church. Much of our so-called evangelism distracts from Christ by focusing on the self. Chuck Colson observes,

> Christian programming melds nicely with the prevailing moods of the culture it purportedly exists to confront. This is not confined to the electronic church. How often do we hear Sunday morning sermons on repentance? Bellah notes in his study that evangelical circles tend to "thin the biblical language of sin and redemption to an idea of Jesus as the friend who helps us find happiness and self-fulfillment." This cheerful accommodation of a self-oriented culture may well be why the church is unable to make a substantive difference in the world.[7]

The apostle Paul warned against giving people what they want instead of what they need. "The time is coming," he told Timothy, "when people will not put up with sound doctrine, but having itching ears, they will accumulate for themselves teachers to suit their own desires, and will turn away from listening to the truth and wander away to myths" (2 Tim 4:3-4). Evangelicals read this warning and feel that it does not pertain to them, because they adhere to "sound doctrine." But as Kenneth Myers reminds us, "Idols and myths can take the form of moods and sensibilities as well as stone and creed, and there are many disturbing signs that many contemporary Christians have made the limited and limiting sensibility of popular culture their own."[8]

It appears that we've become susceptible to the idolatrous moods of novelty, sentimentality and subjectivism. Churches now compete, not only among themselves but with popular culture, in a mood-producing quest for warmth and excitement. They are caught up in providing a diet of entertainment that does not satisfy the need for spiritual nourishment. It does not deepen worship, strengthen the family, encourage spiritual disciplines or commend social justice.

In a consumer-oriented environment it costs money to compete. The first concern for ministry is, invariably, how much it will cost. Can we afford it? Money and ministry are inextricably linked in the market-driven church. It is normal in the American church to think of money as limiting or accelerating ministry. Without money, it appears, our hands are tied.

Think of it! God's great work of salvation is at the mercy of the economy. Perhaps part of the lesson Jesus had in store for Philip and us was that God's work is not threatened by the economy. That, in fact, the power of Christlike compassion is recession-proof. It cannot be hindered by depression, devaluation of the dollar, unemployment and other economic factors.[9]

Jesus is not suggesting to Philip that money has no place in the economy of ministry. Throughout the Gospels, Jesus has much to say about sacrificial giving and the spirituality of stewardship. Here, however, his questioning of Philip not only serves to define the legitimate need and Philip's obligation to meet that need, independent of limited

102 ■ SELLING JESUS

financial resources, but also refocuses Philip on God's work. Ministry is not just a human endeavor, pursued humanistically, but a spiritual endeavor, pursued in partnership with God, even when its goal is meeting physical needs.

*2. From performance to proclamation.* Meeting people's needs, as anyone in ministry can attest, can be a dangerous endeavor. Defining people's real needs is only half the battle. Even when genuine human needs are met, delivering people from false expectations and dependencies is an ongoing, necessary work.

On full stomachs, the people were ready to make Jesus king "by force" (Jn 6:15), so he withdrew into the hills by himself. The people were longing for a political messiah who would provide peace and prosperity, and Jesus fit the bill. He performed to their expectations and then some. Who wouldn't want a miracle-working problem solver on the throne of one's own making?

Christian counselors, pastors, providers, musicians and teachers face this dilemma all the time. The work of meeting people's needs can easily become a performance trap. What began as gifted service becomes an ego-gratifying performance. Under the pressure of a pleased constituency, the best intentions for Christian service may be distorted into the creation of a personality cult.

Jesus resisted this, but many of us do not. The power to meet people's needs goes to our heads, and we become infatuated with our own performance. We end up needing to be needed. Our success leads to more control rather than greater service. Instead of withdrawing to serve people better, we gravitate to center stage. It helps to have people around us calling it "leadership" when in fact it is showmanship. We become professional need-meeters, making a good living meeting the needs of people who treat us like kings as long as we perform according to their expectations.

Jesus walked out of the performance trap by insisting on the truth.

The need for food was significant, but not singular. If Jesus had met only this basic need, he would have been guilty of kingdom negligence and spiritual malpractice.

Meeting people's physical and emotional needs are essential expressions of Christian obedience and love, but offering what I have heard pastors call "a dog-and-pony show" or "a song and dance" is not. Jesus pressed on in a strategic move to transform felt-need expectation. He called the miraculous feeding a "sign," or a pointer, and confronted the crowds with the fact that their interest in him was only because their stomachs were full.

He persisted in using their felt need as a "bridge" to a greater truth. "Do not work for the food that perishes," he said, "but for the food that endures to eternal life, which the Son of Man will give you. For it is on him that God the Father has set his seal" (Jn 6:27).

The majority of the people seem to have been either disinterested or confused by Jesus' "Bread of Life" discourse. There is no hint that they expected Jesus to do anything more than meet their immediate felt need. Judging from the negative feedback Jesus received, his insistence on proclamation was not an effective marketing strategy. The people were either unable or unwilling to make the transition from a physical, tangible product to a spiritual, abstract subject.

The surest way to kill a performance is to demand something from the audience that they're unprepared to give. Jesus' proclamation required serious reflection. This was necessary if the people were interested in understanding what he had to say. But then, as now, serious reflection was not popular.

In fact, the chances of an audience's interacting with a communicator seem higher in a pretelevision oral culture than in today's American culture. We assume that in an ancient oral tradition, thought set the pace of communication, but in today's oral culture the speed of the speaker's articulation is set by the automatic teleprompter or the restlessness of an audience.

Television has had a profound impact on serious communication. Living in a television culture has made communication not easier but more difficult. Quentin Schultze observes,

Most viewers do not approach the TV set with the desire to be challenged intellectually, religiously, or morally. Americans expect and want television principally to entertain them. And by "entertainment" they mean leisure-time fun or diversion; more than anything else they want to be relieved from the boredom of free time and diverted from the stress of the real world. William Stephenson appropriately locates television viewing in the realm of human play. His point is that viewers turn on the tube with playful expectations. This is considerably different from the way an individual might worship, read Scripture or participate in Bible studies.[10]

Television watching is so pervasive that it shapes the way we listen to all communication. If we attempt to communicate the way Jesus did in the Bread of Life discourse, we may find it even more difficult. The temptation is to think that we no longer need to present a serious, abstract message. Sound-bite theology, Christian comedy and heart-moving anecdotes are sufficient to get the message out. But the substance and pattern of Jesus' communication argue against this temptation.

Several important observations can be made in this second stage of felt-need transformation. Although Jesus used simple words, he gave them a complex, abstract thrust, requiring careful reflection from his hearers. He used a simple, graphic visual aid, devoid of religious jargon, and proceeded to develop the "true bread from heaven" theme in a thought-provoking, conceptual way.

"Abstract" is a pejorative term in modern communication. An abstract sermon is the opposite of interesting, exciting and practical. By abstract we usually mean communication that is cold instead of personal, theoretical as opposed to life-related and obscure rather than focused. Such communication is rightly criticized.

Today, however, all serious conceptual thinking and thought-provoking communication faces the danger of being dismissed as "abstract." Unless meaning is immediately accessible, even to the casual hearer, the communication is suspect. To compensate for this criticism, contemporary public discourse substitutes sarcasm for irony, humor for intensity and "thinking by number" for reflection. Preference is given to diagrams over metaphors and graphics over concepts. Not only has thinking become human-centered, but it has become literalistic and light-hearted.

When I talk with my children, I am reminded that thinking conceptually is an acquired skill. Children do not automatically process abstract concepts. They are more attuned to the moment than to meaning. My six-year-old wants to know, "What do I do now?" rather than "Who am I?" Children are more preoccupied with feeling good than with understanding goodness. They understand what hurts long before they contemplate suffering. Their ability to think conceptually, to rise above the immediate, tangible, temporal fact and embrace a larger truth, is a measure of their maturity.

A nihilist or a gnostic may discount the continuum of meaning from the tangible to the intangible, from the material to the spiritual, from the visible to the invisible, but thoughtful people have always understood meaning across the board. A mature person expects to think deeply and feels cheated by the communicator who goes for the tears instead of the brain.

Given the resistance to serious conceptual thinking, it's not surprising that many churches and preachers are judged in the family forum by children rather than by parents. How children feel about a sermon carries increasing significance in a culture striving to be as people-pleasing as possible. If a preacher is a hit with young people, chances are that he'll be successful with their parents.

In the past, parents were encouraged to discuss adult messages with their children in order to facilitate spiritual maturity. Not any more; now they laugh together over the same jokes.

Another important aspect of Jesus' proclamation was his reliance upon the power of God to convince and convict his listeners. "Everything that the Father gives me will come to me, and anyone who comes to me I will never drive away" (6:37). "No one can come to me unless drawn by the Father who sent me, and I will raise that person up at the last day" (6:44). Jesus' reliance upon the Father recognizes the difficulty people have in moving from immediate felt needs to spiritual needs. There was no thought in Jesus' mind that a "command performance" would move the people from popular opinion ("Who does he think he is? We know his parents!") to a solid confession that he is the Bread of Heaven, giving life to the world. Jesus purposed to press the truth well beyond popular appeal and conceptual comfort.

Perhaps too little of today's preaching relies on the sovereign will and power of God for effectiveness. Not only attention spans have been conditioned by thirty-second commercial messages; the presentation of the gospel has been as well. Messages are purposefully kept light and simple, humorous and anecdotal, in order to keep the audience. But this way of keeping the audience may end up losing the audience. The audience never becomes a congregation. The weekly sermon designed for unchurched Harry never makes the transition from performance to proclamation. Harry may feel better, but he remains spiritually unchanged.

The market-driven church stresses the immediate accessibility of every aspect of the Sunday sermon to everyone in attendance. This goal rules out the use of such terms as *redemption, election* and *predestination*. It minimizes theological reflection and close exegesis of biblical texts. It discourages references to church history and key theologians such as Augustine, Luther and Calvin. And it tends to individualize and privatize Christian truth every week in order to make the gospel immediately relevant.

The case for sensitivity to the hearer is a strong one, and the case against religious jargon, pedantic and doctrinaire sermons, and history lessons in the pulpit is a necessary corrective. But an uncritical acceptance of an "accessibility strategy" can impair rather than enhance the proclamation of the gospel. It can dilute the truth rather than develop the truth in penetrating ways.

Besides, much of what the marketing church believes is accessible to the unchurched is in reality very foreign! The vocabulary of the market-driven church—words such as *faith, trust, forgiveness, acceptance* and *love*—is understood in popular culture in ways radically different from the gospel of Jesus Christ. These words that sound so simple may, in fact, be more difficult to communicate clearly and biblically than theological words and concepts such as *atonement, sanctification* and *the kingdom of God.*

For years thousands of American Christians have felt that the simplest evangelistic line they could use was, "God loves you and has a wonderful plan for your life." Given the fact that most people do not know who Jesus is, do not understand the meaning of God's love and have no idea of the significance of the phrase "a wonderful plan for your life," this line, which appears so understandable, can be totally misunderstood.

Jesus took up the challenge to provoke the minds and penetrate the hearts of a reluctant and distracted audience, not through a performance but through the proclamation of the Word of God.

*3. From casual to intense.* In the third stage of communication, Jesus reiterated his message and further intensified it (Jn 6:53-58). Instead of weakening his approach under the pressure of rejection, he grew more explicit, as if to clarify where his listeners stood. He insisted on elaborating powerful metaphors to the breaking point of listener credibility. His transformation of felt needs went further than even many of his disciples could accept.

Jesus' "marketing strategy" (if that is an appropriate term) is diametrically opposed to the strategy proposed by church marketers. Instead of carefully working his audience, making sure everybody kept up and nobody was turned off, Jesus deliberately shocked and challenged. He actually forced his listeners to decide either for or against him by the power of his words and the intensity of his analogies. Without clarifying definitions and careful explanations, he focused the Bread of Life and Passover lamb metaphors upon himself. He could not have been more serious in separating the opinionated from the committed.

Very truly, I tell you, unless you eat the flesh of the Son of Man and drink his blood, you have no life in you. Those who eat my flesh and drink my blood have eternal life, and I will raise them up on the last day. For my flesh is true food and my blood is true drink. (6:53-55)

Some were angry, others were offended; nobody found the message easy. Jesus had managed to alienate just about everybody. The sobering truth in this extended discourse is that the gospel is radical communication, unsuited for neatly contrived worldly categories and self-help comfort zones. The seriousness of the cross hangs over everything Jesus said.

Jesus plunged his audience into truth too deep for humanistic consumption. The ocean of God's truth can be overwhelming apart from the grace of God. But ocean depth has always characterized God's Spirit-filled pastors and theologians. Augustine, Luther, Calvin and Edwards preached the Word of God with a sense of power and mystery. They did not interrupt the momentum of the truth with endearing human-interest stories and tension-releasing humor. They were seriously intense about proclaiming the Word of God. Church history's greatest theologians proclaimed the Word of God as if they were sailing a great ocean spreading to a limitless horizon of God's truth. There was no end to exploring God's truth or delving into its depths. By contrast, today's market-driven pastors invite people poolside to wade in the shallow end. No diving is allowed, and the purpose is recreational.

Before Augustine became a Christian, he instructed students in the ancient art of rhetoric. Respected by many as a master of communication technique, Augustine focused his efforts on delivering a carefully nuanced, refined performance. But he changed after his conversion. Peter Brown observes, "For Augustine . . . rhetoric had consisted of polishing an end-product, the speech itself, according to elaborate and highly self-conscious rules. It ignored the basic problem of communication: the problems faced by a man burning to get across a message, or by a teacher wanting his class to share his ideas. Immediacy was Augustine's new criterion. Given something worth saying, the way of saying it would follow naturally, an inevitable and unobtrusive accompaniment to the speaker's own intensity."[11]

Augustine learned well from Jesus' example. The power and immediacy of "Thus says the Lord" eclipsed the art of rhetoric. Instead of a neatly stylized, well-packaged "talk" that could be praised and forgotten almost simultaneously, Augustine expounded the Bible with emotional feeling and intellectual force. He believed it was his high calling to nurture his congregation in the knowledge of the Word of God, "welding . . . form and content in the heat of the message."[12] Augustine loved the intensity of the Old Testament prophets. "He saw in the prophets, above all, men like himself: men with a message to bring home to a whole 'people'—'a hammer shattering the stones.' "[13]

In an essay titled "A Genius and an Apostle," Søren Kierkegaard complained that many of the preachers in his day were "affected."

Their intensity was artificial. "It is bad enough," Kierkegaard wrote, "the way they talk in a sugary voice and roll their R's like foreigners, and wrinkle their brow and use violent gestures and ridiculous poses. But even more pernicious is that their whole way of thinking is affected. Preachers have become like foolish parents who have to beg, plead, and promise to get their children to obey them."[14]

Kierkegaard believed that the power of the Word of God was not enhanced, but obscured, by the eloquence or brilliance of a genius. He maintained a qualitative difference between a genius and an apostle. A genius is respected for his brilliance, the command of his intellect, the inventiveness of his mind and his quick assimilation of facts. A genius is an innovator whose abilities are clearly superior to others'. The apostle's value, on the other hand, resides not in his abilities but in the call of God upon his life to proclaim the truth of God. We do not listen to Jesus, Kierkegaard contended, because he was clever or eloquent, but because he was wise—wise with the wisdom of God. We respond to him because his words are true.

In the Bread of Life discourse, Jesus felt it was better to turn people off with metaphor and mystery than lead people on under false pretenses. His radical transformation of felt needs was bound to offend some, even as it was powerful to help others.

As the apostle reminds us, to those who are being saved the gospel is the fragrance of life, but to those who are dying it is the smell of death. Nobody in the New Testament ever heard a casual, laid-back, easygoing gospel. The gospel they heard from Jesus and the apostles was a blend of compassion and conviction, delivered with life-and-death seriousness. Holy intensity provoked thought, generated hostility and compelled commitment. Popular rejection was predictable, but the power of their passion for truth prevailed. The thousands who had eaten miraculous bread and thrilled with the prospects of a popular messiah dwindled down to only a few, but the few who remained would end up turning the world upside-down.

*4. From excitement to fellowship.* In the fourth and final stage of communication, Jesus focuses the attention of those who remain with a question: "Do you also wish to go away?" (Jn 6:67).

All the hype and commotion of need-meeting on a massive scale had come down to a small group of disciples. Instead of facing the throng, he faced twelve men, one of whom would betray him. Jesus resisted the temptation to reduce the gospel to popularity by sacrificing either integrity or intensity. He insisted on letting the truth run its course, even though that meant rejection and confusion. Unlike so many who have a popularly based ministry, Jesus judged effectiveness by faithfulness. He refused to develop separate tactics, one to grow the church numerically and another to grow the church spiritually. He was prepared not only for people to walk away but for people to go deeper. His strategy transformed an audience into a congregation.

Are we prepared to communicate the gospel as Jesus did? Can we compassionately meet people's needs, declare the gospel without manipulation or compromise and nurture those who are willing to distinguish between a felt need for positive affirmation and the spiritual need for deliverance?

The market-driven church tends to believe in "public opinion as an arbiter of truth." Nathan Hatch writes, "By thus admitting the sovereignty of the audience, evangelicals, knowingly or not, undercut the structure that could support critical theological thinking on the level of a Jonathan Edwards or a John Wesley."[15] The American church has uncritically, and in some cases unconsciously, accepted a division between evangelism and discipleship (preaching the gospel and Christian theology) that divides confession and commitment. For the sake of "seeker sensitivity," preaching remains superficial, with thousands of confessing Christians fed a weekly diet of entry-level evangelism. There is little time or energy for developing any consistent pattern of preaching the whole counsel of God.

In the Bread of Life discourse, Jesus moved against two tyrannies that continue to threaten the gospel, especially where these tyrannies are seen as signs of success rather than dangers. In the 1800s, Alexis de Tocqueville expressed concern over the "tyranny of the majority." He feared that "serious thinking would be hooted down in the marketplace before it could mature." Though Tocqueville had expected "that great freedom of thought would generate great ideas, he found instead that Americans easily became 'slaves of slogans.' "[16] Rather than risk rejection or negative feedback, the market-driven church gives the majority what they want. Consumer-oriented preaching does very little to transform felt needs.

The second tyranny is described by Eugene Peterson as the tyranny of feelings. Preaching and worship are orchestrated around the emotional needs of the audience. Instead of worship being an emotional outpouring to God in adoration or lamentation, it is an opportunity for the emotional needs of the self to be satisfied. In the market-driven church, people come to church because it is self-satisfying, not because God is worthy of all praise and glory.

A true transformation of felt needs moves people from self-centeredness to Christ-centeredness and from familiarity with Jesus to an intimate relationship with Jesus. Peter expresses well the success of Jesus' ministry in his response to Jesus' question: "Lord, to whom can we go? You have the words of eternal life. We have come to believe and know that you are the Holy One of God" (6:68-69).

In the development of the household of faith, there is a Spirit-led progression from compassion to proclamation and from spiritual intensity to Christ-centered intimacy. Community takes shape as the whole counsel of God takes root. Although this progression may strike many as unreasonable, it is absolutely essential to the integrity of the church.

That is not to say it will be easy. George Barna recognizes this, but he seems unconcerned about incorporating Jesus' pattern of transforming felt needs.

> The commands of Jesus will seem like an appeal to asceticism to most Americans, an unappealing prospect at best. In an era in which we are seeking to build our self-esteem and to feel good about ourselves through conscious, overt acts of generosity and kindness, the hard-line requirements of Christianity will simply be too much for millions of people to accept. They may not vociferously challenge or oppose the Christian life-style and belief structure, but they will dismiss our faith as impractical and unreasonable for today's world.[17]

Barna warns, "We will be tempted to downplay the importance of commitment and obedience. We will be tempted to soften the truth so that a hardened generation will give us a fair hearing."[18] The question is whether Barna and others, in advocating a marketing approach to the gospel, have not already yielded to this temptation. Richard Lovelace proposes a more difficult approach, but one that reminds us of Jesus:

> We may need to challenge more, and comfort less, in our evangelism and discipleship. We need to make it harder for people to retain assurance of salvation when they move into serious sin. . . . We need to tell some persons who think they have gotten saved to get lost. The Puritans were biblically realistic about this; we have become sloppy and sentimental in promoting assurance under any circumstances.[19]

The church cannot afford to feed the insatiable appetite of culturally generated felt needs and remain faithful to its identity and mission. The temptation is strong for the church to prove its attractiveness in secularly defined, socially acceptable ways. But love demands a distinction between self-actualization and Spirit-led confirmation. Our love must abound more and more in depth of insight, so that we can distinguish "the cravings of sinful man" from profound spiritual needs; so that we can discern between the lust of the eyes and the beauty of God's holiness; so that we can understand the difference between boasting of our own accomplishments and placing our faith in God's accomplishments. Taming and transforming felt needs was a prerequisite for Jesus' public ministry and ours.

# 7

# IN
# SEARCH OF
# EXCELLENCE

*The marketplace is now the most widely used system
of evaluation by younger churchgoers.*

LYLE SCHALLER

The West has witnessed the unprecedented downfall of communist ideology and rule in Eastern Europe and Russia. Communism, as a political and economic philosophy, gradually ground to a halt under the burden of low productivity, corruption and confusion. The communist economic system became incapable of meeting even basic human needs. Capitalism, on the other hand, holds an increasingly pervasive hold on the West, not only economically and politically but socially and spiritually as well.

One of the reasons Christians opposed communism is that it reduces the meaning of the person to functional, economic categories. Communist ideology denies not only God but also humanity, made in the image of God. Democracy, many Christians believed, should prevent this depersonalizing economic reductionism.

But now we see that capitalism has seriously encroached on all aspects of American life, to the point that the marketplace dominates nearly every institution and sphere of the culture. Everything seems to get tossed into the capitalistic hopper: political campaigns, personal self-esteem, sports, family life, medicine, education and even the church. There appear to be no institutions strong enough to remain independent from the marketplace. The solidarity of the family is dependent on career success. We pride ourselves not on our familial relationships but on our job performance. Education has become market-driven, so that departments and programs are funded on a revenue-producing basis. Administrative titles reflect this change; "principals" have become "presidents" with heavy responsibilities for fund raising; "deans" have become "vice presidents," managing budgets and programs. Capitalism has turned the university into a corporation and the student into a consumer.

Medicine has become unbelievably entrepreneurial and capitalistic; with one out of every four dollars going to business administration, capitalism has created a complex, bureaucratic system of insurers, investors, managers and profit takers. The consumer mentality, in good old-fashioned capitalistic fervor, has shaped the way we think about friendships. Time is money, and emotional resources are limited; unless we perceive a relationship to be profitable, we are reluctant to "buy in."

Communism has fallen in Russia, but capitalism is soaring in the West, dominating American life and exalting the marketplace to sacred significance.

## The Corporate Challenge
As I pointed out earlier, George Barna distinguishes between the tactics used for growing the church numerically and the strategy used for

developing the church spiritually. The first set of tactics begins with the market-driven church's discovering and defining its market niche. This is followed by determining and then meeting the target audience's felt needs. A third tactical decision calls for the consumer-oriented, market-sensitive church to pursue a standard of excellence drawn from and competitive with the best-run American corporations.

The church of the nineties is encouraged by church marketers to evaluate itself according to the performance standards of the marketplace. The church's administration, facilities, communications, public relations and long-range planning are to be judged by secular criteria. The standard of efficiency, professionalism and quality of IBM, AT&T and Toyota is now used to measure the church.

The rationale for this emphasis on corporate excellence is to impress baby boomers with the same quality of performance they have become accustomed to in the marketplace. "How else are we going to impress the world with Christ?" asks the church-growth consultant.

According to church marketers, Americans feel toward the traditional church the way they felt toward Japanese products in the 1960s. Thirty years ago, Americans poked fun at the poor quality of Japanese manufacturing. "Made in Japan" was synonymous with "cheap." But now it means quality. What Japan did to revolutionize its image in the marketplace—stringent quality control, innovation and performance checks—the church needs to do in order to convince consumers that it can compete effectively for their time and energy. Barna writes:

Perhaps the 90's will enable us to examine quality, rather than quantity, as a better indicator of success and church growth. If the experience of many of today's growing churches is any indication, the best means of gaining quantity is through quality: Americans are irresistibly drawn to those organizations that ooze quality. Given our shifting values, and the peaking interest in excellence and high standards, churches which evoke a sense of quality will be more attractive than those that simply continue to perform their usual routine, oblivious to standards.[1]

One of the ways the market-driven church can impress today's consumer is by becoming "technologically savvy." The new tools for pastoral effectiveness and efficiency include computers, FAX machines and cellular phones. "In a society driven by speed and information," writes Barna, "it is imperative to invest in useful technology. . . . as time goes on, more and more people will expect the Church to at least be in the game technologically. . . . It will be increasingly difficult to convince the unchurched, and those who are questioning Christianity, that our faith is pertinent to the 21st century if the tools of our trade are from the last century." Barna envisions churches incorporating video into their services, faxing bulletins to members in advance of Sunday and setting up computerized spiritual resource centers to provide "easily accessible and pertinent data for spiritual growth."[2]

The church's main competition, according to Barna,

is not with other churches—it is with organizations, opportunities, and philosophies that provide people with an alternative to the Christian life. Our main competition is from organizations like ABC, CBS, Universal Studios, MGM, K-Mart, 7-11, JC Penney, and so forth. . . . How many local churches do you know that are able to compete with the same tough mindedness, the same highly focused sense of purpose, and an equivalent level of professionalism in promoting their ministry (i.e., business) and product as their secular competitors?[3]

The message Barna and others communicate in their church-growth consultations is that unless your church impresses boomers as a well-run company on the cutting edge of innovations and professional competence, it will not be able to compete effectively in the marketplace. They predict a spiritual downturn and an evangelistic "recession" if corporate excellence is not pursued.

It is interesting to see how this emphasis surfaces in the daily routine of church life. Church leaders expend most of their energy on administrative and financial matters. Session, vestry or board meetings are dominated by the business of running the church. More time is spent discussing budget, interest rates, debt reduction, expansion plans and the cost of new programs than dealing with church discipline, worship and spiritual direction.

"Goal-oriented churches," observes Philip Yancey, "usually choose goals that are relatively easy to accomplish: a new building, an increase in size. But Jesus said very little about these goals; he talked instead of unity and love and justice. How well are we accomplishing them?"[4]

Churches striving for excellence do not necessarily translate that concern into meaningful Communion services, consistent church discipline, training in spiritual disciplines, better premarital preparation or more Christ-centered worship. The excellence they seek is, by definition and perception, a quality separate from godliness. A market-driven church in pursuit of excellence may have a very efficient management team, but little heart for world missions. It may have a beautiful sanctuary and a splendid music program, but an audience full of spectators. It may have a large professional staff giving leadership to a full-service church, but offer little pastoral care and spiritual direction.

By distinguishing between tactics that grow the church numerically and strategies that deepen a church spiritually, Barna has separated an objective criterion of success and a subjective criterion of spiritual value. Church marketers do not say that the church can be successful apart from the work of the Holy Spirit and prayer, but they create that impression by defining excellence in terms foreign to the New Testament and familiar to the marketplace.

When Paul said to the believers at Corinth that "all things should be done decently and in order" (1 Cor 14:40), he was focusing on the quality of their church discipline, their use of spiritual gifts, their celebration of the Lord's Supper and the integrity of their worship in a pagan culture. Ironically, church marketers assume success in those very areas that the church has struggled with for centuries. Organizational excellence is promoted, but prayer, authentic spirituality and Christian ethics are assumed.

This market-sensitive, businesslike approach to excellence becomes especially apparent in the expectations placed on the market-driven pastor. The marketing mentality is changing not only the style but also the character of pastoral leadership.

### The Fortune 500 Pastor

Today's counterparts to the nineteenth-century frontier prophets of doom who delivered fiery harangues guaranteed to move the lost to tears are winsome, charismatic, executivelike pastors who exude warmth and success. Known more for their humor than for their spirituality, today's market-sensitive pastors are relationally savvy. They connect with their audiences, articulating the people's hopes and longings better than they can. Instead of eliciting deep feelings of guilt as the old revivalists did, these pastors lift the spirit, promote optimism and make people feel good about themselves. Their style blends vulnerability and empathy with confidence and concern. They are transparent and transcendent, combining personal openness and victory into an image that is both reassuring and compelling.

Pastors are expected to be one-person critical masses, providing the vision, setting the tone and maintaining quality. They are CEOs, visionary team leaders, as much disciples of Peter Drucker as of Jesus Christ. Modern pastors in market-driven churches have an entrepreneurial spirit, a flair for public relations and a gift for inspiring people. They are a cross between an executive and an entertainer, personifying the image of the church and modeling contemporary spirituality. Market-driven pastors, as pictured by Barna, sound like superapostles. They are people of prayer and serious Bible study. They are in tune with the details of the megachurch, but "not bogged down by them."[5] Such a pastor is usually a take-charge, dominant leader, but "ultimately a team player," excellent in delegation and encouragement.[6] These pastors support a broad range of ministries and are models of personal spirituality. Strong pastors are generally agreeable and approachable. They are unfailingly positive and upbeat, but if a situation warrants it, they can be confrontational. They are loving spouses, excellent parents and "involved in forms of ministry other than preaching and administration."[7]

These people have the "gift of visibility," lending "an aura of credibility and significance" to ministries they may not be integrally involved in. They don't seek the spotlight, but they are at the right place at the right time. They are excellent teacher-preachers as well as effective motivators and one-on-one counselors. Their sermons are down-to-earth, practical and relevant. They honestly admit their mistakes, frankly recognize their bad decisions and openly take tough stands. Of course, these multitalented, multigifted pastors have all these qualities without pride or pressure.

With such an impressive list of qualities, is it any wonder that market-driven churches are being built around superpastors? People no longer unite with a body of believers, but pick a church because they like the preaching and personality of a pastor. Denominational affiliation and geographic location mean less and less, while a strong platform ministry and a full-service, felt-need program mean more and more. "Pastors are expected to be informed, articulate, and charismatic," says Leith Anderson. "They are to be as attractive and well groomed as the anchorman on the network news, and they are expected to relate to the peculiarities of the community. They are to attract people, raise money, and expand programs."[8]

I heard a senior pastor of a fast-growing megachurch pray, "Lord, we look forward to your soon return, when you'll be our senior pastor." But in the meantime, the market-driven church is placing a superhuman weight of responsibility on a single person. This is reflected in the "key man" insurance policies that some megachurches have, to cover the church in excess of a million dollars if the pastor should die. Church boards and lending companies fear that if the senior pastor were no longer able to perform his or her duties, attendance and giving would plummet, placing the church in a serious financial crisis. Perhaps such a policy and the fear and insecurity it reflects are signs of the weakness of the market-driven megachurch.

### Counterfeit Excellence

Christians in the marketplace face a tremendous challenge to think and live Christianly in an environment that is foreign to the ways of Christ. A number of years ago, I was involved in a seminary course designed to help business professionals consider a biblical perspective on success, ambition, stress, family life, servant-leadership, economics, unemployment and many other issues related to a Christian work ethic and worldview.

I cotaught the course with Ray Binkley, a Christian brother who was an executive at Shell Oil. Ray was committed to integrating his faith in Christ with his responsibilities in the workplace. In a class of more than forty businesspeople and twenty seminarians, we stressed the need to center on Jesus Christ; to pace ourselves by a rhythm and pattern of worship and devotion; to internalize and apply Jesus' kingdom ethic; to prioritize in practical ways our commitment to the household of faith and to our families; and to live our lives in the light of eternal values and realities.

One of the books we read in preparation for the course was *In*

*Search of Excellence,* by Thomas Peters and Robert Waterman. This popular bestseller illustrated many of the positive, practical things "America's best-run companies" were doing to be successful. But from the perspective of a Christian work ethic, *In Search of Excellence* skimmed the surface. Although the book provided a number of practical, common-sense suggestions for creating a positive, satisfied customer, it failed to deal with marketplace dynamics beyond the issue of managerial style. Doing business the right way involved a concern for quality, quick thinking, flexibility, openness to new ideas, and positive reinforcement of workers and customers.

Corporate excellence, according to Peters and Waterman, means that customers reign supreme and workers feel they are part of a winning team. The atmosphere is upbeat and positive, generating a feeling of excitement and competition. The individual belongs to a successful organization that is open to change and responsive to needs, and has a built-in bias for action.

What is interesting is that the style of doing business proposed by Peters and Waterman is now being implemented by innovative, trendsetting churches. The Peters and Waterman approach to excellence is dominating the managerial style and working objectives of progressive churches aiming to impress baby boomers in terms they can understand. What is good for business is good for the church.

It makes sense that a generation of consumers striving for success in the business world would be impressed by qualities commended by America's blue-chip companies. The question, however, is this: Having accepted the corporate challenge, how does the church implement the dynamic model of the early church in Acts? Does the style of doing business replace the substance of building Christian community? To what extent is the church countercultural? How does Jesus' "Sermon on the Mount" message impress laptop-toting executives looking for a church home? Is excellence determined by marketplace standards or a biblical view of holiness?

Certainly the church can learn from the business community better ways to manage its organization and improve communication, but I believe business has more to learn from the church than the church has to learn from business. If corporate excellence is the goal, where do servant leadership, spiritual gifts, sacrificial giving, quiet meditation and the kingdom ethic fit into the picture?

The issue for the church is the temptation to accept a criterion of excellence that is determined by the marketplace rather than the Word of God. People may be impressed with excellent facilities, a state-of-the-art sound system, decision-making flexibility, executive-style leadership, professional nurseries, efficient organization and a warm, user-friendly atmosphere, but will they be impressed with our daily and corporate worship of God, our grasp of the whole counsel of God, our simple lifestyles and our sacrificial commitment to Christ's command to go and make disciples of all nations?

## Biblical Models of Excellence

Peters and Waterman evaluate what works for America's best companies, but the Bible proposes an alternative model for excellence that was meant to work for the body of Christ. As the disciples walked through Herod's temple, they were impressed, remarking on "how it was adorned with beautiful stones and gifts dedicated to God" (Lk 21:5). Jesus did not share their enthusiasm for Herod's standard of excellence. Everything that awed the disciples was destined for destruction: "As for these things that you see, the days will come when not one stone will be left upon another; all will be thrown down" (Lk 21:6).

It was not "what" but "who" that impressed Jesus. The poor widow escaped everybody else's notice but his. He saw her drop into the offering "two small copper coins," which amounted to everything she had.

Perhaps we are so familiar with the account that we ignore the obvious model of excellence Jesus commends. He valued the heart of this poor widow far more than Herod's world-class facility.

Biblical models of excellence provide a distinctive picture of "quality control." There is a striking contrast between George Barna's *Marketing the Church* and J. I. Packer's *A Quest for Godliness*. How does the Puritan model of a holistic, holy lifestyle compete with baby boomer expectations? Does the Puritans' holy passion for spiritual renewal compare favorably with American evangelicals' search for excellence? Jim Packer commends the Puritans as a historic model of maturity for contemporary Christians. "Maturity is a compound of wisdom, goodwill, resilience, and creativity. The Puritans exemplified maturity; we don't. We are spiritual dwarfs. A much travelled leader, a native American, has declared that he finds North American Protestantism, man-centered, manipulative, success-oriented, self-indulgent and sentimental, as it blatantly is, to be 3,000 miles wide and half an inch deep."9

A market-driven, consumer-oriented standard of excellence distorts rather than enhances a Christ-centered philosophy of ministry. Vernon Grounds compares the world's standard of excellence to Christ's standard:

Worldly success is success judged without reference to God or eternity. Spiritual success is judged by God, success from the perspective of eternity, success without reference to the world's evaluation. . . . The church has allowed the world to impose on Christian service standards of success which are utterly non-biblical; and when I talk of the church in this context I mean American evangelicalism. . . . the right kind of thinking plus the right programming and motivating plus the right battery of techniques will change any failure into shining success. . . . I am honestly afraid that American evangelicalism is guilty of idolatry. It is bowing down, if I may borrow a biting phrase from philosopher William James, before the bitch goddess of success. It is worshipping at the shrine of sanctified (or unsanctified) statistics. . . . As disciples of Jesus Christ, too many of us are sinfully concerned about size—the size of sanctuaries, the size of salaries, the size of Sunday Schools. Too many of us are sinfully preoccupied with statistics about budgets and buildings and buses and baptisms. I say it bluntly: too many of us American evangelicals are worshipping the bitch goddess of success.[10]

The goal of excellence sought by the market-driven church may have its place in helping to produce a smooth, well-run operation, but this goal is secondary to the primary concern of holiness. In fact, many of the positive qualities sought by church marketers, such as excellence in communication, financial accountability, sensitivity to people, flexibility and long-range planning, are products of spiritual maturity and godliness. It is ironic that today's church should be enamored with business-school strategies for conflict management, personnel evaluations and consumer profiles when they have had immediate access to the biblical wisdom literature and the pastoral epistles.

As in the days of King Josiah, when the Book of the Law was found after years of neglect and ignorance, the modern, market-driven church may have to rediscover the Bible. Our neglect of the Word of God is subtle and deceptive. Our Bible is not buried in the janitor's closet; it is prominently displayed on the church altar and located in every pew rack. But we use it in token fashion. Congregations informed by daily Bible reading and prayer have been replaced by biblically illiterate audiences. Pastors use Scripture as a platform from which to launch Christianized self-help talks. Therapy is disguised as theology, and preaching is promoted as performance. It is amazing how much of the Bible is becoming inappropriate for consumer consumption on Sunday mornings. The market-driven church has turned to new oracles for inspiration and direction. Israel flirted with the Baal fertility cult; we are tempted to follow the latest trends in management and therapy.

An alternative to corporate excellence is the higher, more comprehensive goal of the beauty of holiness. The biblical concept of beauty goes beyond marketplace standards. Executive-style excellence is similar to modern conceptions of beauty. Quality is measured on the surface—a matter of appearance and style, statistics and budgets. Biblical beauty, on the other hand, is inclusive and comprehensive, involving the totality of meaning, from architecture to administration, from celebrating Communion to counseling, from accounting to attitudes, from relationships to convictions.

The words of David show a passion for excellence unfamiliar to many modern Christians.

One thing I asked of the LORD,
that will I seek after:
to live in the house of the LORD
all the days of my life,
to behold the beauty of the LORD
and to inquire in his temple. (Ps 27:4)

The desire "to behold the beauty of the Lord" was a prayer to center the totality of life in God. It was more a spiritual and theological reality than what we narrowly call an aesthetic experience. Beauty was found in the integration and fittedness of every aspect and event in the scope of life. For the Israelite, loveliness extended to the exodus, Zion and the Day of the Lord. The Hebrew concept of beauty involved substance and structure more than style and finish. William Dyrness writes, "It is difficult for us to imagine such a grand harmony and wholeness, for we have gotten out of the habit of seeing things as a whole. . . . We no longer understand the role beauty properly ought to play in our fragmented lives. So beauty only expresses our isolation.

It does not provide the delight and comfort of integration."[11]

The market-driven church isolates component parts that go into making an attractive, user-friendly church, such as a music program, youth program and child care. Each aspect is usually dependent upon a professional staff member and budget and evaluated according to how well run and popular the program is. The overall operation is administered by professionals who are concerned to keep all the programs running efficiently and effectively.

But the whole is not necessarily centered in Christ or integrated in a Christian worldview. Generally, the product is customer satisfaction, not spiritual maturity. Individuals within the megachurch may earnestly serve Christ and have a profound spiritual impact, but they do so in a fragmented structure that tends to isolate workers and capitalize on their efforts. The church itself remains largely impersonal and disconnected, so that it becomes increasingly difficult to get volunteers. Serving in such a church can be like working for a major corporation, where individual effort is specialized and carried on without a sense of the whole operation. Worship and spiritual growth then become features of the user-friendly church rather than the focus.

A return to the biblical standard of beauty and excellence would insist on an integration of Christ-centeredness, biblical integrity and authentic Christian living in every aspect of the church program. The modern market-driven, user-friendly church can be well run and very popular, but may lack the essential character of a household of faith.

Dyrness's explanation of the biblical concept of beauty clarifies what the Bible means by excellence:

In the Old Testament an object or event is not beautiful because it conforms to a formal ideal but because it reflects in its small way the wholeness of the created order. Something is lovely if it displays the integrity that characterizes creation and that in turn reflects God's own righteousness. . . . The key to much of modern aesthetics is the autonomy of form and the purity of aesthetic experience. In the Old Testament the contrast that we have seen is not between beauty and ugliness but between beauty in its setting, serving God's purpose, and beauty that is prostituted by leading away from the just order that God intended.[12]

An illustration of this distinction between marketplace excellence and biblical beauty can be seen in how churches plan Christmas music programs. Though the content of these programs is usually theologically sound and evangelistically important, the performance may take on the aura of a stage production. Musicians, many of whom profess no relationship with Christ, are paid for their services. Publicity and ticket sales attract an audience that anticipates an aesthetic experience, but not necessarily a worship experience. Choir members are trained in musical technique, but the meaning of the text is unexplored. Applause, not prayer, is the fitting response to this gigantic expenditure of time, money and energy. If this work is not integrated into the devotional life and biblical understanding of the choir and the congregation, the Christmas musical program becomes just another special feature in a busy holiday schedule. Holy work is unintentionally profaned in an effort to stage a performance and please an audience.

Another illustration of the dichotomy between modern excellence and biblical holiness can often be found in youth ministry. Today's high-energy, excitement-filled youth program creates a context of amusement, attracting young people from negative peer-group pressure and directing them to a felt-need gospel. Invariably, success is measured in numbers—both the number of kids attending and the number of activities sponsored. Quantity, it is thought, signals quality. Youth ministry often takes on a life of its own, independent of ministry to young children, parents and the elderly. It becomes a paraministry within the church, reinforcing peer pressure and generational boundaries. The activities are often expensive: a winter ski camp, a summer excursion to Florida, weekly meetings at McDonald's, concerts and movies.

Few seem to question whether a church youth ministry should be built on amusement and activities. Excellence requires it, but does godliness? What is the spiritual impact of these programs on our young people? Do they deepen their character and encourage reflection and understanding? Why is it that so many of our young people go away to university without understanding their faith or themselves? Is there not a gap between marketplace excellence and the beauty of holiness when it comes to youth ministry?

I am especially grateful when an adult comes alongside one of my children and seeks to guide him or her in the faith. A simple, consistent commitment to teach a junior-high or senior-high Sunday-school class can have a profound spiritual impact on young people. An adult who is not afraid to be serious about the Word of God and who demonstrates a genuine concern for young people can be used of God to nurture faith and change lives.

I remember the year Ed Hamilton taught my son Jeremy's sixth-grade Sunday-school class. I wondered how Ed would be received. He was a quiet-spoken, calm man who taught recreational therapy at the university. He was known to the boys as Dr. Hamilton, and although people treated Ed as if he could do anything, he was paralyzed from the waist down and dependent on a wheelchair. Ed's temperament, Ph.D. and wheelchair seemed to make him an unlikely candidate for teaching an elementary boys' class. To the casual observer, Ed did not convey the attractive image necessary to excite the kids and make the class a success.

As the weeks passed, however, Jeremy grew in his respect for Ed. He began recounting to us the discussions they had in class about the Word of God. He was learning from Ed's Christ-centered character, and he looked forward to their time together.

Because Dr. Hamilton took his class seriously, the boys began to take him—and Christ—seriously. Excellence was achieved through Ed's Christ-centered commitment to the boys rather than in a culturally predictable way.

Market-driven standards of excellence produce youth programs with attractive externals, while the beauty of holiness builds a youth ministry on solid cross-generational relationships centered in Christ. Fun activities and exciting events are still part of the program mix, but they don't dominate and overpower young people, leaving them incapable of focusing their minds and hearts on the Word of God.

Youth ministries cannot afford to direct their ministry to the lowest common denominator out of fear that young people will be turned off or will criticize Bible study as boring. Their mission is not to attract people to an exciting program but to draw young people to Christ's love and build disciples.

Compared to the beauty of holiness, corporate excellence is counterfeit. It is an inadequate standard for judging the quality of a church or ministry. Excellence can be achieved by a market-sensitive church that never actually becomes a household of faith. As in Herod's temple, the external display can be remarkable, but the character, holiness, integrity and authenticity of the church as the body of Christ can be weak.

### The Quest for Godliness

The modus operandi for ministry depends upon God for both its power and its pattern. Jesus taught his disciples to pray, "Your will be done, on earth as it is in heaven" (Mt 6:10). God's people were not meant to be innovators, rushing to meet people's felt needs by setting up a golden calf. They were expected to wait obediently upon God, even when it seemed the world was passing them by.

This does not mean that faithfulness needs to divorce effectiveness, or that the church denies the benefit of administrative strategies, sociological awareness and psychological insight. All truth is God's truth. But if the benefits of these new techniques and perceptions are to be realized, they need to be sanctified through prayer and an understanding of God's Word. The church's immediate acquisition of worldly trends and skills, such as marketing, without spiritual scrutiny is like dispensing drugs without the regulation of the Federal Food and Drug Administration or the approval of a doctor.

If we expect to guard the church from secularization, our pastors' conferences and church-growth consultations will have to weigh evangelistic strategies and management theories more for their theological value than for their utilitarian merit. "Wherever pragmatism exists in the church," John MacArthur warns, "there is always a corresponding de-emphasis on Christ's sufficiency, God's sovereignty, biblical integrity, the power of prayer, and Spirit-led ministries. The result is a man-centered ministry that attempts to accomplish divine purposes by superficial programs and human methodology rather than by the Word or the power of the Spirit."[13]

A good test for whether a church is opting for executive-style excellence or the beauty of holiness is how people view their pastor. If they think their pastor could be CEO of a major corporation, anchor the evening newscast or run for political office, they probably have confused a successful public image with spiritual leadership. When people say their pastor could do anything he sets his mind to, they misunderstand the power and wisdom of Spirit-guided leadership and place their confidence in a multitalented individual.

I am not suggesting that Christians who are business executives or politicians should be any less spiritual or Christ-centered than pastors. What I am saying is that our view of the pastor is too humanistic. We judge a pastor more by personality and worldly competence than we do by faithfulness to the holy vows of ordination.

If we are serious about the pursuit of godliness, we will need a new kind of pastoral role model: pastors who do not cater to worldly respectability but contend for the faith with maturity and passion in the midst of a relativistic, secularized culture. They will refuse to do our work for us and won't allow us to experience Christ vicariously through their spirituality. They will join with other mature men and women of God to help a congregation of believers grow up in the faith and reach out in Christ's love.

### The Prophet-Pastor

John the Baptist provides an outstanding alternative model to the market-driven pastor. John's philosophy of ministry included a defined task, a definite message and a dogmatic assertion. Cultural expectations did not confuse him or sidetrack him from his ordained task. He was sent to prepare the way of the Lord. His awareness of God's sovereignty, confirmed by his family's spirituality and reinforced by his own life-preparation, led him to understand and work out his divine call with singular devotion and passion. His self-image was rooted in disciplined communion with God and was resistant to either popular or negative feedback. "I am the voice of one crying out in the wilderness, 'Make straight the way of the Lord' " (Jn 1:23).

John's message was stated in concise, powerful lines—bold assertions uncommon in the religious discourse of his day. His passion was for righteousness, not excellence. "Repent, for the kingdom of heaven has come near" (Mt 3:2). "Here is the Lamb of God who takes away the sin of the world!" (Jn 1:29).

John's preaching was also in sharp contrast to that of many contemporary religious communicators. He was unlike the relational speaker who is conversational and humorous as well as vulnerable and uplifting. Neither was he bombastic or egocentric. John was not a pulpit-pounding type, employing an inflammatory rhetoric and self-exalting style. John fit neither category. He was intense, passionate, exhortative and decisive. He declared, "Thus says the Lord . . ."

"What about the pastor who preaches a biblical and prophetic message people don't want to hear?" asks Leith Anderson. "No longer can he expect the congregation to stick around and listen. They will leave and go where they can hear a message they like."[14] Fred Smith laments the fact that "one of the jobs of a 'successful' pastor is to make the irresponsible comfortable."[15] Thankfully, this was not John's philosophy of ministry. He would not have accepted those who receive praise for being vulnerable and empathic at the expense of declaring the Word of God. He would rather be known for declaring the truth of God than be praised for sensitivity to people's feelings.

It appears that Martin Luther, the great reformer, followed in John's tradition: "To take no pleasure in assertions is not the mark of a Christian heart; indeed one must delight in assertions to be a Christian at all. . . . let me say here that by 'assertion' I mean staunchly holding your ground, stating your position, confessing it, defending it, and persevering in it unvanquished. . . . Take away assertions and you take away Christianity."[16]

What if we were led by prophet-pastors instead of popular pastors? This new pastoral role model would alter the congregation's expectations, revolutionize the current terms of pastoral endearment and help restore the biblical responsibility of being a pastor. Instead of hiring a pastor to meet my personal needs, conduct ceremonies and run the church, what if we called a prophet-pastor to lead us in worship and train us in the whole counsel of God? This would remind us that the Word of God, delivered authoritatively and powerfully, is at the center of the pastoral vocation. And that this Word, preached and practiced, prepares God's people for works of service, which include the full range of ministry needs: comfort and companionship, works of compassion, helpful counsel, church administration and world mission.

## Centering on Christ

There was no arrogance in John's assertiveness. There was an essential self-effacing quality to his ministry that did not come at the expense of truth. He was bold and authoritative, yet he did not draw people to himself. He led people to Christ. He repeatedly affirmed, "I am not the Christ" (Jn 1:20-23; 3:27-28).

What John was not was just as important as what he was! He accepted no title and claimed for himself no biblical fulfillment. A self-pronounced claim to be a prophet on the order of Elijah would have confused his message and distracted from his purpose to announce the Messiah. If John had maintained that he was the prophet described in Deuteronomy 18:15, the people's attention would have shifted to himself and away from the one who was to come. Controversy and debate would have ensued about John's identity.

John refused to debate about himself. He purposely remained humbly indifferent and noncommittal regarding his Elijah-like role. Who he was, was nothing; what he came to do and whom he came to introduce were everything. John left it to Jesus to confirm his special calling. He refused to reinforce spiritual weakness by allowing people to exalt him. He reiterated, "I am not the Christ!"

"He's no Pied Piper," complained one parishioner of his pastor. "We need someone who can attract people." The man who leveled this criticism at his faithful pastor had forgotten not only the biblical responsibility of a pastor but also the story of the Pied Piper.

A certain musician came to town, offering to rid the town of rats for a fee. The town leaders agreed, and the Pied Piper played his magic flute and led all the rats out of town. His task completed, he requested his reward, but the town withheld the promised payment. So in revenge, he blew his magic pipe and enticed the children of the town to a cave in the side of a hill; once they had entered, he sealed the cave, closing the children in forever.

John was not a Pied Piper, leading people astray. He was self-effacing and Christ-focused. His effectiveness was evident in Andrew's transition from John to Jesus. And the one line that was particularly instrumental in shifting attention away from John and toward Jesus was the absolutely crucial truth—that Jesus is the ground of our redemption, the means of our salvation: "Here is the Lamb of God who takes away the sin of the world."

Vernon Grounds tells a story that illustrates this well.

One night Arturo Toscanini, perhaps the most dynamic of modern maestros, led a simply spine-tingling rendition of Beethoven's immortal masterpiece [the Ninth Symphony]. The audience went wild. People clapped, whistled, and stomped their feet. Toscanini bowed and bowed and bowed. He signaled to the orchestra, and its members stood to acknowledge the wild applause.

Eventually, of course, the pandemonium began to subside, and with the ebbing applause as background, Toscanini turned and looked intently at his musicians. With almost uncontrollable emotion he exclaimed, "Gentlemen! Gentlemen!" The gentlemen in the orchestra leaned forward to listen. Why was the maestro so disturbed? Was he angry? Had somebody missed a cue? Had the orchestra flawed the performance?

No. Toscanini was not angry. Toscanini was stirred to the very depths of his being by the sheer magnificence of the Beethoven music. Scarcely able to talk, he said in a fierce whisper, "Gentlemen, I am nothing." (This was an extraordinary admission since Toscanini was blessed with enormous conceit!)

"Gentlemen," he said, "you are nothing!" (That was not exactly news. The members of the orchestra had often heard the same message in rehearsal!)

"But Beethoven," said Toscanini in a tone of adoration, "is everything, everything, everything!"[17]

John did not see himself as the Elijah-like prophet but as a friend of the bridegroom, whose sole purpose was to attend to the bridegroom, to wait and listen and prepare for the bridegroom to come. The bride belongs to the bridegroom. In the same way, the joy of a pastor is seeing people united to Christ. "He must become greater; I must become less." "Being a pastor that satisfies a congregation," remarks Eugene Peterson, "is one of the easiest jobs on the face of the earth, if we are satisfied with satisfying congregations." But that is not what pastors and spiritual leaders are called to do. "We set out to risk our lives in a venture of faith. We have committed ourselves to a life of holiness."[18] The simple question pastors need to ask themselves distinguishes clearly between counterfeit excellence and holiness: "Is my primary orientation God's grace, his mercy, his action in Creation and covenant? And am I committed to it enough that when people ask me to do something that will not lead them into a more mature participation in these realities, I refuse?"

Making the decision to pursue godliness and the beauty of holiness, rather than executive-style excellence, will refocus our attention on the biblical pattern of ministry and the ancient tools of ministry. We may, in fact, use computers, FAX machines and video equipment, but the strength of our ministry will lie in praying the psalms, knowing how to worship and understanding the Word of God. Our management style will reflect Christ's sacrificial service more than the latest trends in how to "handle" people. Our success will be measured in spiritual maturity, compassion for others and the integrity of the household of faith.

The call for holiness will not excuse administrative sloth and shoddy ministry. It will transform the principles and priorities of excellence from a corporate standard to a biblical standard. The language of "success" will change from image to character, from achievements to relationships, from productivity to maturity and from management to mission.

# 8
# THE
# HOUSEHOLD
# OF FAITH

Unless the LORD builds the house,
those who build it labor in vain.
Unless the LORD guards the city,
the guard keeps watch in vain.

**PSALM 127:1**

It's hard to argue with success. To question the wisdom of the market-sensitive, market-driven church sounds like sour grapes or a narrow, "puritanical" spirit coming from someone who cannot adjust to the fresh winds of the Spirit.

I am confident that the Lord will build his church with or without American innovations and prophetic critiques. And I am certain that the Lord will guard and preserve his church so that "the gates of Hades will not prevail against it" (Mt 16:18). He will even save us from our grand designs and great expectations.

God does not need people to critique the initiatives of sincere, well-intentioned believers. But the Lord does call his followers to discernment. As the apostle Paul prayed, our Lord's desire is that "your love may overflow more and more in knowledge and full insight to help you to determine what is best, so that in the day of Christ you may be pure and blameless, having produced the harvest of righteousness that comes through Jesus Christ for the glory and praise of God" (Phil 1:9-11).

Spiritual direction is often a call back to the basic faith and to practice that shapes and strengthens the church as the body of Christ. Nothing new is said, nothing that most believers do not already know. Discernment is not so much an intellectual exercise as a discipline of faithfulness. It is like sifting through a pile of brightly colored junk mail and coming up with a letter from a friend that deserves to be read, reread and answered.

Church growth is dependent not upon buying a new product but upon participating more fully and faithfully in God's work through prayer, worship and obedience. "Unless the LORD builds the house, those who build it labor in vain" implies a partnership between the master craftsman and the apprentice. We have been called into a working relationship with the Lord Jesus modeled on the relationship between the Son and the Father. "My Father is still working, and I also am working. . . . Very truly, I tell you, the Son can do nothing on his own, but only what he sees the Father doing; for whatever the Father does, the Son does likewise" (Jn 5:17, 19). No grand designs, only simple humble, faithful service.

We need to clarify in practical ways God's expectations and ours. Straightforward spiritual direction frees us from unnecessary guilt and clarifies the will of God.

The church suffers from well-intentioned believers who follow the example of the world when they do "God's work." Unwittingly they apply a Tower of Babel philosophy to the work of God. "Come, let us build ourselves a church, with programs that will attract great numbers and make a name for ourselves." It is difficult to know whether it is entrepreneurial zeal or evangelistic zeal that has created a market for church-growth geniuses who promote conferences that lay out the secrets of success for your church to copy. Patterned more after sales conventions than Bible conferences, these motivational seminars promise great things. Without a hint of humility, they advertise and promote their success.

"Discover the principles and strategies that have caused this church to grow from one family to 4,400 in attendance in its first eleven years, while at the same time starting sixteen daughter churches. Come and see for yourself what others are talking about." Sincere pastors read this and wonder whether their church can become as successful. Maybe they are missing some key to church growth that, if discovered, will turn their situation around.

It is important to remind ourselves from beginning to end that the work of the church is God's work. We can claim it as our own only to the extent that we follow God's lead. This means that our work and effort must always draw wisdom and energy from God. What holds true for our salvation is also true for the church. In Ephesians 2:8-10, we are warned against turning "God's work" into an expression of self-effort. There is no ground for boasting. We are apprentices to the Master Craftsman.

## Holy Ambition

The alternative to both the traditional church and the market-driven church is a Christ-centered household of faith—a community of sojourners who are in the world but not of the world. These modern-day pilgrims are focused on Christ and shaped by the cross. They take the Word of God seriously and have a deep passion for Christ. There is a Spirit-guided, rather than market-driven, rhythm and pattern to their lives, which includes worship and service, rest and action, solitude and community, meditation and mission.

Holy ambition discerns the difference between targeting a market niche and discovering Christ's mission for the church. It distinguishes between consumer-oriented felt needs and deep-seated spiritual needs. Holy zeal knows the difference between corporate excellence and the beauty of holiness. It warns against a pastor-centered church and favors a ministry-centered church. It resists the temptation to substitute attractive peripherals for penetrating fundamentals. Spiritual maturity knows that "when misdirected zeal replaces holy ambition, we embark on a long obedience in the wrong direction."[1]

The household of faith fights spiritual inflation by stressing the unity of confession and commitment in a community of disciples. While market-driven churches are attracting thousands of individuals because of the personality of the "key man," felt-need satisfaction and special features, the household of faith is trying to work alongside Christ, following a pattern of conviction and obedience that has been in place since the apostles.

There is no shelf-life limitation to the principles described in Acts. These qualities are preserved indefinitely, as long as they are handled faithfully. The early church offers today's American church a character description, not a formula for success. Devotion to the Word of God and corporate worship created a community that nurtured personal spiritual growth and an openness to the supernatural work of God. Material and emotional needs were met in a community that was God-centered. The early Christians focused on Christ daily, enjoyed one another's company and demonstrated the love of Christ in society. Luke tells us that "day by day the Lord added to their number those who were being saved" (see Acts 2:42-47).

The household of faith does not need a new campaign, a new program, a new cutting-edge strategy for marketing the church to baby boomers. What it needs is a renewed commitment to the whole counsel of God, to Christian friendship and body life, to prayer and worship, to baptism and the Lord's Table, to meeting the needs of the poor and to reaching all people everywhere for Christ.

The issue for the church of the nineties is not that we become more innovative but that we become more prayerful. We need not assume new and unbiblical pressures. John Maxwell, pastor of Skyline Wesleyan Church in San Diego, expresses a common fallacy: "When churches run out of new ideas or new programs, they stop growing." The result of this kind of thinking has been numerical growth at the expense of spiritual growth. The demand for novelty and excitement ends up distracting churches from becoming a household of faith.

We are called not to invent but to remember. Keeping up with the competitive marketplace is becoming a burden. As one pastor put it, "My church expects a new five-year plan every eighteen months."

Too many misconstrue Proverbs 29:18, "Where there is no vision, the people perish" (KJV), to mean, "Where there is no expansion plan, building program, family-life center, self-help sermons, the church dies." Yet the true growth of the church is not dependent on a public relations vision, but on our faithfulness to the Word of God. "Where there is no revelation, the people cast off restraint; but blessed is he who keeps the law" (NIV).

Instead of market sensitivity we need spiritual sensitivity. The church does not need twenty-four-hour-a-day marketing agents competing for attention in the world as much as it needs men and women of God whose quiet lives, solid convictions and Christlike character authentically represent the gospel.

**What Does the Lord Require?**
The simple commands are always the hardest to obey—loving each other in Christ, offering hospitality, serving those in need, keeping sexually pure, remaining faithful in marriage and resisting the love of

money. It seems easier for a church to build a multimillion-dollar family life center than to be a Christian family.

If we are to challenge nominal Christianity and move beyond an adolescent faith, we need to heed the exhortation of the writer of Hebrews and pay more careful attention to what we have heard, so that we do not drift away. The early church grew through the guidance and power of the Holy Spirit. There was a sacrificial commitment to the integrity of the Word of God and a consistent moral and ethical challenge to the surrounding culture. There were no artificial inducements or secular attractions to entice the masses. The early church had impact because of the penetrating truth of the gospel and the power of transformed lives centered in Jesus Christ.

More than seven hundred years before Christ, the prophet Micah sought to guide the people of God. He lived in an era, like our own, when there was great confusion over what God truly wanted from his people.

Micah recites all that God has done for Israel: liberating them from Egypt, guiding them in the wilderness, meeting their needs. But with all that God has done for the people, they remain sinfully confused about what God wants in return. Micah satirizes their confusion by putting himself in their shoes and asking,

> With what shall I come before the LORD,
> and bow myself before God on high?
> Shall I come before him with burnt offerings,
> with calves a year old?
> Will the LORD be pleased with thousands of rams,
> with ten thousands of rivers of oil?
> Shall I give my firstborn for my transgression,
> the fruit of my body for the sin of my soul? (Mic 6:6-7)

Micah took the people's woeful spiritual ineptitude and insensitivity to ludicrous extremes. Only the rich would entertain the idea of offering a valuable year-old calf for a burnt offering. But no one would ever think of offering thousands of rams or ten thousand rivers of oil. Would God be impressed with such a lavish religious performance? Was God so inhumane and greedy as to require them to pour out all their energy and resources in some spectacular display of religious hype? Micah mocks the people for thinking of God as the ultimate consumer, entertaining the strictly forbidden sacrifice of firstborn children. Israel was taking its cues from the surrounding pagan culture and disdaining the obvious ways of pleasing God.

Today's church is asking what is expected, just as the Israelites to whom Micah was writing did. Instead of asking, "What is an impressive sacrifice?" we are asking, "What is effective evangelism?" The borrowed pagan rituals of sacrifice that impressed the Israelites are replaced today by innovative, capitalistic styles of evangelism. Instead of living the gospel, we are trying to sell it to consumers who are hungry for a transcendent experience. Instead of ten thousand rivers of oil, we have a multimillion-dollar church campus, billed as a full-service church, offering shopping-mall variety and programmed to meet an array of felt needs.

Unconsciously the evangelical church has slid toward New Age thinking, catering to the self as god, by offering an impressive range of what we call "necessities" rather than "sacrifices." There may be a place for great nurseries, climate-controlled facilities, practical, uplifting, "fix-it" sermons, plenty of accessible parking, a family-life center, support groups, bowling teams, Christian rock concerts, hymn sings and plenty of crowd-pleasing events. But in the process of impressing God and people, we have forgotten what really matters in church growth and what is required in building a household of faith.

Today's church is innovative, efficient, hyperactive and high-energy—but spiritually lazy. "Sloth is doing nothing of what we were created to do as beings made in the image of God and saved by the

Cross of Christ," says Eugene Peterson. "Sloth is laziness at the center, while the periphery is adazzle with a torrent of activity and talk."[2] Like the Israelites in Micah's day, we're anxious to please God; but much of what we want to do for God, God doesn't want done. The American church prefers to be overactive, overworked, overinvolved and financially overextended. Ironically, this seems easier to do than to humble ourselves and return to the basics of prayer, worship, service and love. Through a profound rationalization, the American church is tempted to substitute marketing complexities for spiritual simplicity.

The French Christian Jacques Ellul offers penetrating insights into the relationship between theology and sociology. His critique of propaganda serves a double duty. Much of what Ellul says about propaganda applies equally as well to marketing the church. Where the word *propaganda* falls in the following quotes from his book *Propaganda,* I have substituted the word *marketing.*

"[Marketing] has the freshness and novelty which correspond to new situations and gives man the impression of having invented new ideals. It provides man with a high ideal that permits him to give in to his passions while seeming to accomplish a great mission." As with propaganda, marketing helps to reassure the Christian that he is "in full accord with his group and with society, and fully adjusted to his environment, as well as purged, at the same time, of his pangs of conscience and personal uncertainty."

Marketing is the tool that will do church growth for us. It offers "a simple and clear explanation of the world . . . to be sure, a false explanation far removed from reality, but one that is obvious and satisfying." Marketing hands us "a key with which [we] can open all doors; there is no more mystery; everything can be explained, thanks to [marketing]." The marketer "experiences feelings of mastery over and lucidity toward his menacing and chaotic world, all the more because [marketing] provides him with a solution for all threats and a posture to assume in the face of them."³

Contrary to the popular church-growth perspective, marketing strategies are not necessary to contextualize the gospel for the baby boomer. What is required for effectiveness and faithfulness is what Micah wrote centuries ago to a generation consumed with showy externals and religious felt needs:

He has told you, O mortal, what is good;

and what does the LORD require of you

but to do justice, and to love kindness,

and to walk humbly with your God? (Mic 6:8)

The prophets are, at times, aggravatingly simple. Their critiques are full-blown, colorful descriptions of hypocrisy, distortions and rationalizations, but their bottom-line prescriptions are stark and straightforward. We cannot get lost in a list of steps or confused with intricate techniques. There is no mystery involved in taking the Word of God seriously, no magic in determining to be God-centered in worship.

But I doubt that the people were satisfied with Micah's exhortation. Very likely they rejected his admonition, claiming he had it all wrong. Where Micah saw sinful compromise, they claimed common-sense convenience and compatibility with the surrounding culture. What exactly did Micah mean by justice and mercy, anyway? Perhaps they criticized the prophet for not being practical enough. But the real problem is that doing justice, loving mercy and walking humbly with God is *too practical.*

The seventeenth-century Puritan pastor Richard Baxter called for spiritual renewal and authenticity in the church. He proposed a very simple method for accomplishing this: teach people the fundamentals of Christian character and faith through personal tutorials and examinations. He emphasized the responsibility of spiritual leaders "to catechize and to teach personally all who are submitted to their care." This method originated out of Baxter's frustration with professing Christians who had listened to his preaching for years, but remained spiritually immature and indifferent.

It would be difficult to find a pastor who valued preaching more than Baxter, but he concluded that many churchgoers were either unable or unwilling to grasp the truth of the gospel through public preaching:

> Let them that have taken most pains in public, examine their people, and try whether many of them are not nearly as ignorant and careless as if they had never heard the gospel. For my part, I study to speak as plainly and as movingly as I can . . . and yet I frequently meet with those that have been my hearers eight or ten years, who know not whether Christ be God or man, and wonder when I tell them the history of his birth and life and death as if they had never heard it before. . . . I have found by experience, that some ignorant persons, who have been so long unprofitable hearers, have got more knowledge and remorse in half an hour's close discourse, than they did from ten years' public preaching.[4]

Baxter admitted there was nothing new or complex about this strategy. His plan for renewal was basic. "I wonder at myself," he wrote. "Why was I so long held back from doing so obvious and vital a duty?" He admonished pastors, "Make it your great and serious business to teach the fundamentals of the faith to all the members of your congregation by these private tutorials."[5]

Richard Baxter was not interested in a doctrinaire faith but in a living, applied faith that would take seriously the whole counsel of God. He advocated a disciplined faith, the opposite of a laid-back, easygoing, connect-the-dots, paint-by-number Christianity. His holistic, integrated approach knew no division between evangelism and discipleship. Outreach and edification went hand in hand. He wanted his people to learn their theology by heart, internalizing Christian conviction and actualizing Christian practice.

We do not need to go back to the seventeenth century for exhortations to biblical integrity. Prophetic voices resound today as well. "The most dangerous thing we can do is to return to spiritual worship," writes Warren Wiersbe.

It would mean the end of the personality cults that have invaded the church. It would also mean the end of the "Christian consumerism" that has so twisted our sense of spiritual values. I have no doubt that the church that returned to true worship would lose people—"important people"—and probably have to make drastic cuts in the budget. But then something would happen! A beautiful new sense of spiritual reality would result, with people glorifying God instead of praising men. There would be a new unity among God's people, no matter what label they might wear; and the divisive spirit of competition would gradually vanish.[6]

What the Lord requires of us is something fundamentally life-fulfilling and enriching. It is neither manipulative nor mechanistic. It is not something we can engineer or manufacture. Church growth is not subject to mass production. It is not something we can control, predict or determine. It is related to Christian obedience and faithfulness, but even then the body of Christ is always reminded that "unless the Lord builds the house, those who build it labor in vain."

Instead of being pushed and pulled by consumer expectations and church-growth trends, we are invited to participate in the divine patience. Our waiting and watching always precede working. We are confident that God goes before, preparing, convicting and comforting, so that the gospel can take root. Farming, not retail, remains the working analogy for Christian mission.

**Providence Versus Progress**
Psalm 127 is one of the psalms of ascent, a collection of psalms that

were sung and prayed as sojourners headed to Jerusalem to celebrate the Passover. It was prayed by pilgrims, not religious tourists. This psalm helps us to appreciate the dimensions and dynamics of the household of faith.

The trip to the temple in Jerusalem was a faith journey undertaken by Israelite families as an expression of discipline and devotion. Through this physical exercise and spiritual experience, people centered their families and personal lives on the reality of the living God and reminded themselves of the source of their blessing and the object of their hope.

The psalm captures the totality of life: family and society, vocation and children. No wonder the Hebrews saw themselves first in terms of community and only second as individuals. They prayed for their families, "Unless the LORD builds the house . . ." They prayed over the city, "Unless the LORD guards the city . . ." They prayed for work and rest: "It is in vain that you rise up early and go late to rest, eating the bread of anxious toil; for he gives sleep to his beloved." They prayed for children: "Sons are indeed a heritage from the LORD, the fruit of the womb a reward."

They centered their worship on the living God; they centered their lives on the work of God. This was a faith journey of families. They were not family-centered but God-centered. They worshiped and served with their families. Peterson correctly observes, "The character of our work is shaped not by accomplishments or possessions but in the birth of relationships."[7]

What a beautiful picture of holy ambition. The Lord's work invites investment in people, not possessions. It is shaped by truth, not techniques. The healthy development of a family is a fitting analogy to the growth of a church. The birth of a child causes us to marvel at the creative power and handiwork of God. Even the act of love and a difficult pregnancy do not lessen the strong feeling that we are participating in a work far beyond ourselves. The sinister deception of the new reproductive technologies is that we would somehow believe that we manufacture, control and engineer life when all we are doing is discovering, in greater detail, the work of God.

It is tempting to do whatever we can do to bring about the desired effect, whether we want children or church growth. But the means as well as the ends must be considered from God's will.

As many married couples have experienced, the desire for a child is very strong. Ginny and I were childless, so we booked an appointment with a fertility expert at Mt. Sinai Hospital in Toronto. The doctor described various therapies and concluded that artificial insemination (AI) was our best option. The procedure involved collecting and then implanting my sperm in Ginny's womb.

We had discussed AI before going to the specialist. A few Christians had told us they thought the procedure was wrong because it was "unnatural" and "artificial." Their advice was, "If God wants you to have children, God will provide." Yet we saw nothing biblically wrong with facilitating the fertilization process in this manner, so we followed through with the visit to the specialist.

After the doctor politely explained the procedure, he added that since my sperm count was low it would be advisable to use sperm from a third party (AID). Ginny and I looked at each other. I turned to the doctor and somewhat shyly said that we believed AID was a violation of God's perspective on marriage.

Even though it was the same procedure, we reasoned that the source of the sperm makes a great moral difference. By introducing donor sperm, we would be tampering with the sanctity of marriage—not in the form of an adulterous relationship but in a more subtle way that was still contrary to the meaning of the marital bond as described in the Bible.

We were not prepared for what followed. The doctor's professional tone abruptly changed. With a sharp glance to Ginny, he angrily asked, "Do you want children or don't you? I'll do anything for my patients." Then he glared at me: "I don't care if people think I'm a pig. I'll do whatever my patient wants or needs."

The conversation ended, and we left. We had come to a line we believed we should not cross.

This incident is a parable that applies to church growth. The American church is tempted to build the church through clever marketing strategies that will attract people. Predictable growth is something we can arrange for and produce if we satisfy religious consumers' expectations by meeting felt needs and creating a user-friendly atmosphere. Marketing offers tactical approaches to numerical growth that stand independent of being a household of faith and growing in the grace and knowledge of the Lord Jesus Christ. It is efficient and convenient, yet it subtly violates the will of God by reinforcing self-effort: human-centered, materialistic church growth.

I wonder whether the first people who prayed and sang Psalm 127 were tempted to measure the significance of their trip in terms of the number of miles they traveled to Jerusalem. Perhaps they thought that the more miles covered on the journey the greater their spirituality. Judging from the psalm, however, the spirituality of the pilgrims was measured not in achievement but in dependence upon the living God. They did not have a quantifiable understanding of success, but a qualitative understanding of relationship with God. They were not preoccupied with their work and effort. The pilgrimage was not at the center; the Lord was at the center.[8]

Calculating successful church growth numerically is equally misleading. It has as much to do with pleasing the Lord as an odometer ticking off the miles to Jerusalem.

In fact, we have large churches that probably need to become smaller if they are to experience church growth. Spiritual growth

152 ■ SELLING JESUS

would shrink, not expand, many of our churches. Those who have seen God at work building and nurturing the household of faith do not calculate spirituality in statistics but in worship. Their work is on the periphery; God's work is at the center. Everything they do is in response to God's plan and initiative, and they behold his glory.

Psalm 127 insists on a perspective in which our effort is at the periphery and God's work is at the center. I agree with Lesslie Newbigin's observation: there is "an underlying Pelagianism which lays too much stress on our own activities and is too little controlled by the sense of the greatness and majesty and sufficiency of God."[9]

Christopher Lasch argues that Americans are too optimistic. We believe in being positive even when the situation calls for sober concern and difficult change. "American historical writing," says Lasch, "takes little account of the possibility of tragedy—missed opportunities, fatal choices, conclusive and irrevocable defeats. History has to have a happy ending."[10] My concern is that this naive optimism and belief in progress will get in the way of a serious reappraisal of how the evangelical church approaches church growth. The emphasis on marketing the church that we have examined is "a kind of Christian activity which only thinly masks a lack of confidence in the sufficiency of God."[11]

Long ago, Richard Baxter affirmed a distinction, which still stands today, between Christian hope and human optimism.

By showing people the certainty and the excellence of the promised joy, and by making them aware of the perfect blessedness in the life to come in comparison with the vanities of the present life, we may redirect their understanding and affections toward heaven. We shall bring them to the point of due contempt of this world and fasten their hearts on a more durable treasure. This is the work we should be busy with both night and day. For when we have affixed their hearts unfeignedly on God and heaven, the major part of the min-

istry is accomplished. All the rest will follow naturally.[12]
My prayer is that the American church will restore its belief in divine providence and reaffirm its willingness to participate in divine patience. Our "staying power" depends upon God, not ourselves. We live in the light of the most real world, filled with the vision of God's presence and the hope of receiving an unshakable kingdom. We wait in good faith for an enduring city, committed to the destiny of salvation history and the discipline of daily obedience.

I have a dream that the body of Christ in America can recover spiritual depth, moral integrity and ethical maturity. I believe that with God's help we can get beyond felt-need distractions and concentrate on the pressing spiritual needs of the human condition. And that by grace we can endure disgrace, with a vision not only of our responsibility but of God's holy glory.

# PRACTICAL SUGGESTIONS FOR THE HOUSEHOLD OF FAITH

*1. In an effort to take God more seriously than budgets and buildings, plan a monthly two-hour prayer session and Bible study for elders and ministry leaders.* Focus on the church as a household of faith. Evaluate the biblical meanings of success, servant leadership and worship.

*2. Center the life of the church on worship.* Make worship the chief goal of missions, Christian education, youth ministry and Sunday services. Discover how God-centeredness is the most effective tool in evangelism, fellowship, disciplemaking and mission. Bring all those who are involved in directing the worship services together for a monthly prayer and planning session.

*3. Begin worship with quiet meditation and personal prayer.* Allow this time of silence and prayer to move worshipers from the noise and commotion of busy schedules. This simple act goes against the grain of our culture. Educate the congregation to see the importance of preparing for worship by coming on time and participating in prayer and praise.

*4. Emphasize the importance of the sabbath principle for the rhythm and pattern of family and personal life.* Reclaim Sunday from sports and shopping for the sake of spiritual growth, fellowship and worship. This can be done positively through teaching and personal example, rather than dogmatically and legalistically. Do not fill Sunday with church committee meetings.

5. *Nurture a congregation of worshipers by weaning people from a spectator mentality and a performance expectation.* Move away from entertaining features, musical performances and humor as a crowd-pleaser. Look at worship as an integrated whole, rather than component parts. Diminish the master-of-ceremonies role in favor of a liturgy that focuses on God through great hymns, songs of praise, prayer, preaching and Holy Communion.

6. *Learn to pray the psalms and practice the spiritual disciplines.* If we are left to ourselves, our prayer life is often flat and anemic. Prayer requests degenerate into a list of physical ailments. Praying the psalms is an education in genuine spiritual expression—richer praise, deeper lament and mature dependence. It is the best antidote to clichéd praise. Use the psalms to focus meditation, to guide the call to worship and to give depth to corporate prayer.

7. *Restore to preaching its true purpose of guiding people in the whole counsel of God.* Overcome the unwarranted distinction between preaching and teaching. The Bible is far more than a starting point for a series of illustrations and anecdotes. Preaching should be biblical teaching that moves, comforts, instructs and challenges the body of believers. Authentic preaching will also be effective in answering the questions and concerns of earnest seekers.

8. *Permit seekers easy access to information about the church.* Designate key people, who are gifted in building relationships, to help befriend newcomers. Create a nonpressured approach to new people that will avoid both forced friendliness and uncaring anonymity. Personally invite seekers to a home fellowship group or a special gathering where they can meet the elders and pastoral team. Show people

love, but do not chase them or cling to them.

*9. Integrate the proclamation of the Word of God on Sunday mornings with small-group ministries and youth programs.* Not only is good preaching shaped by the Word of God from beginning to end, it also shapes the biblical community. Develop a daily devotional guide on biblical texts related to the preaching ministry.

*10. Start early in training children to hear and interact with the Word of God.* Move away from amusing young people and socializing adults. Encourage young people and adults to prepare for Sunday school by working through a Bible-study lesson. This will increase thoughtful participation and deepen the church's appreciation for the Word of God.

*11. Use the sacraments of the church, baptism and Holy Communion, in a theologically thoughtful way.* Whether it adheres to believer's baptism by immersion or infant baptism, the church has the responsibility and the opportunity of affirming the meaning and integrity of personal commitment to Christ. The sacraments should be preserved from a perfunctory administration. Elders or deacons should meet with individuals and families who desire baptism and use this as an occasion to strengthen the faith.

*12. Educate people in a disciplemaking process that begins early and extends through life.* Show practical interest in how the Christian life is worked out in the home and at work. Special studies for Christians in business, law, science or medicine will help people to think Christianly about their vocations.

*13. Prepare high-school students to understand their culture from a Christian worldview.* Using the Word of God, interact with the events, philosophies, music and personalities of the culture. Students should have at least a basic understanding of God and humanity, good and evil, pain and suffering, salvation and death. Carefully work through one of the Gospel accounts to develop a clear understanding of the life and purpose of Jesus.

*14. Reverse the trend that makes the pastor more a manager than a theologian, more an administrator than a spiritual director, more a master of ceremonies than a worship leader.* Under the auspices of the elders or deacons, delegate administrative responsibilities to lay leaders. Develop a team ministry approach that relies on the spiritual gifts and commitments of mature believers. Encourage lay leadership while preserving the authority and leadership of the pastoral team.

*15. Expect the household of faith to evangelize through its counter-cultural distinctiveness.* Remember, it is God's called-out, visible community, set apart to be salt and light in a dark world. Refuse to accommodate by catering to the world's expectations. When the church gathers, it is for the purpose of glorifying and praising God. Weddings and funerals are not social services to the community; they are God-centered worship services. If they cannot be done in integrity, they should not be done.

*16. Stimulate Christian fellowship through an intentional Christ-centeredness.* Bonding among Christians is not a socializing function but a spiritual exercise. People are drawn together in the bond of Christ as they participate in his mission. Fellowship groups should be organized around prayer and Bible study. Encourage small groups to focus on a particular ministry that they can share in.

*17. Offer a training course for prospective leaders that reviews the biblical expectations of leadership in the household of faith.* Develop a mentoring relationship between mature, gifted leaders and potential leaders. In all areas of church life, appoint leaders who are holy in character and spiritually wise.

*18. Encourage membership in the body through a nurturing program that stresses a clear confession of faith in Christ and an understanding of personal commitment and responsibility within the church.* Do not push membership to raise a number; instead, provide membership to develop solidarity in Christian growth and commit ment.

*19. Practice preventive and corrective church discipline.* Compare people's concern for their physical health with their spiritual health. Give people an annual "spiritual," administered by the spiritual leadership of the church. This would involve nonthreatening conversations with church members about their walk with God, their spiritual growth and their ministry responsibilities. The long-term practice of such dialogs will help people know that their personal growth in Christ is valued by the church.

*20. Do not motivate people with guilt or challenge them with flattery.* If after prayer and thoughtful encouragement a person does not respond to a ministry opportunity, leave the matter with God.

*21. Confront, rather than overlook, sinful behavior.* Do this in a manner and spirit true to the counsel of the Word of God. Express a genuine concern for individual believers and the integrity of the household of faith, so that Christians will not be left in their sin and the witness of the church will not be distorted.

*22. Network with believers from other cultures and with missionaries.* Develop a direct relationship with a church or churches in another culture. This may mean a close relationship with an inner-city church, where members of your church serve that body in teaching tutorials, coming alongside leaders or meeting physical needs. Personalize your friendship and concern for believers in other cultures by focusing your support and prayer.

*23. Pray to the Holy Spirit for an openness and sensitivity to the dynamic of God's work in your church.* Expect God to work in people's lives, drawing them to Christ and building them up in the faith. Allow God to show you ways of making your church an authentic household of faith.

*24. Remember that the life of the church and the growth of the body*

*are in God's sovereign care.* It is our responsibility to actively participate in the divine patience—waiting, watching, working in the tradition and example of our Lord Jesus Christ. Seek first his kingdom and
his righteousness, not your market share. Make it your goal to do
everything in the character of Jesus and to the glory of God.

# Notes

## Chapter 1: Church Growth Made Easy

[1]George Barna, *The Frog in the Kettle: What Christians Need to Know About Life in the Year 2000* (Ventura, Calif.: Regal Books, 1990), pp. 22-23.

[2]Ibid., pp. 44, 47, 60.

[3]Ibid., pp. 62-63, 153.

[4]Stanley Hauerwas and William H. Willimon, *Resident Aliens* (Nashville: Abingdon, 1989), pp. 46-47.

[5]Søren Kierkegaard, *Concluding Unscientific Postscript to the "Philosophical Fragments,"* in *A Kierkegaard Anthology,* ed. Robert Bretall (Princeton, N.J.: Princeton University Press, 1946), p. 194. The Kierkegaard quotes that follow all come from this same page.

## Chapter 2: Marketing the Church

[1]Richard D. Dinwiddie, *"Messiah:* Behind the Scenes of Handel's Masterpiece," *Christianity Today,* December 17, 1982, pp. 12-20.

[2]See Nathan Hatch, "Evangelicalism as a Democratic Movement," *The Reformed Journal,* October 1984, p. 12.

[3]George Barna, *Marketing the Church: What They Never Taught You About Church Growth* (Colorado Springs, Colo.: NavPress, 1988), p. 41.

[4]Ibid.

[5]Ibid., p. 23.

[6]Ibid., p. 14.

[7]Ibid., p. 12.

[8]Ibid., p. 37.

[9]Doug Murren, *The Baby Boomerang* (Ventura, Calif.: Regal Books, 1990), p. 35.

[10]Ibid., p. 45.

[11]Barna, *Marketing the Church,* p. 59.

[12]George Barna, *User Friendly Churches* (Ventura, Calif.: Regal Books, 1991), p. 23.

13Barna, *Marketing the Church*, p. 32.
14Ibid., p. 50.

### Chapter 3: The Traditional Church
1Murren, *Baby Boomerang*, p. 95.
2Ibid., p. 196.
3Barna, *Marketing the Church*, pp. 21, 55.
4Ibid., p. 28.
5Ibid., p. 22.
6Tom Wolfe, "Tom Wolfe's Walk on the Wild Side," interview by Alvin P. Sanoff, *U.S. News & World Report*, November 23, 1987, p. 57.
7Murren, *Baby Boomerang*, pp. 38, 168.
8Ibid., p. 77.
9Eugene Peterson, *Reversed Thunder* (San Francisco: Harper & Row, 1988), p. 55.
10Eugene Peterson, *A Long Obedience in the Same Direction* (Downers Grove, Ill.: InterVarsity Press, 1980), p. 169.
11Peterson, *Reversed Thunder*, p. 55.
12Murren, *Baby Boomerang*, p. 35.
13Barna, *User Friendly Churches*, p. 22.

### Chapter 4: The Target Audience
1Lyle Schaller, quoted in Mark Galli, "Learning to Be Some Things to Some People," *Leadership*, Fall 1991, p. 37.
2Barna, *Marketing the Church*, p. 42.
3Murren, *Baby Boomerang*, p. 262.
4Leith Anderson, *Dying for Change* (Minneapolis: Bethany House, 1990), p. 13.
5Christopher Lasch, *The Culture of Narcissism: American Life in an Age of Diminishing Expectations* (New York: Norton/Warner, 1979), p. 137.
6Murren, *Baby Boomerang*, p. 101.
7Paul Tournier, "Exploring the Inner Dynamics of Success," *Leadership*, Winter 1981, p. 42.
8Daniel Yankelovich, *New Rules: Searching for Self-Fulfillment in a World Turned Upside Down* (New York: Bantam Books, 1982), p. 8.
9Ibid., p. 187.
10Paul C. Light, *Baby Boomers* (New York: W. W. Norton, 1990), p. 204.
11Murren, *Baby Boomerang*, p. 52.

[12]Ibid., p. 52.

[13]William A. Dyrness, *How Does America Hear the Gospel?* (Grand Rapids, Mich.: Eerdmans, 1989), p. 56.

[14]Light, *Baby Boomers,* p. 10.

[15]Ibid., 21.

[16]Harry Blamires, *The Christian Mind* (London: SPCK, 1978), p. 156.

[17]Ibid., pp. 8-9.

**Chapter 5: Meeting Felt Needs**

[1]Anderson, *Dying for Change,* p. 95.

[2]George Barna, "The Church of the '90s: Meeting the Needs of a Changing Culture," *Reformed Theological Seminary Journal,* September 1990, p. 11.

[3]Ibid.

[4]Volvo North America Corporation, 1991.

[5]Barna, *Frog in the Kettle,* p. 164.

[6]Yankelovich, *New Rules,* p. 8.

[7]Murren, *Baby Boomerang,* p. 101.

[8]Ibid., p. 103.

[9]Ibid.

[10]Neil Postman, *Amusing Ourselves to Death: Public Discourse in the Age of Show Business* (New York: Penguin Books, 1985), p. 28.

[11]Ibid., pp. 27-28.

[12]Ibid., p. 156.

[13]Gustav Niebuhr, "Mighty Fortresses: Houston's Second Baptist Uses Secular Attractions to Bring in a Huge Congregation," *The Wall Street Journal,* May 13, 1991, pp. A1, A6.

[14]Ibid., p. A1.

[15]Barna, *Frog in the Kettle,* pp. 92-93.

[16]Peterson, *Reversed Thunder,* p. 142.

[17]Hauerwas and Willimon, *Resident Aliens,* p. 39.

[18]C. S. Lewis, *Surprised by Joy* (London: Fontana, 1959), p. 176.

[19]Charles Colson, "Barbarians in the Pew," *Jubilee,* July 1988, p. 7.

[20]Hauerwas and Willimon, *Resident Aliens,* p. 33.

[21]Stephen Arterburn and Jack Felton, *Toxic Faith: Understanding and Overcoming Religious Addiction* (Nashville: Thomas Nelson, 1991), p. 41.

**Chapter 6: Transforming Felt Needs**

[1]John Stott, "Secular Challenges to the Contemporary Church," *Crux,* Sep-

tember 1991, p. 2.

[2]C. S. Lewis, *The Weight of Glory and Other Addresses* (New York: Collier, 1980), pp. 3-4.

[3]Peterson, *Long Obedience,* p. 12.

[4]Yankelovich, *New Rules,* p. 239.

[5]Os Guinness, "Mission in the Face of Modernity," in *The Gospel in the Modern World: A Tribute to John Stott,* ed. Martyn Eden and David F. Wells (Downers Grove, Ill.: InterVarsity Press, 1991), p. 95.

[6]John Stott, *Christian Mission in the Modern World* (Downers Grove, Ill.: InterVarsity Press, 1975), pp. 29-30.

[7]Colson, "Barbarians in the Pew," pp. 7-8.

[8]Kenneth A. Myers, *All God's Children and Blue Suede Shoes: Christians and Popular Culture* (Westchester, Ill.: Crossway Books, 1989), p. 87.

[9]See Richard Halverson, "Counting the Cost of a Church Rich in Resources," *Christianity Today,* July 17, 1981, pp. 42-45.

[10]Quentin J. Schultze, *The Business of Popular Religion: Televangelism and American Culture* (Grand Rapids, Mich.: Baker Book House, 1991), p. 190.

[11]Peter Brown, *Augustine of Hippo* (London: Faber & Faber, 1967), p. 256.

[12]Ibid.

[13]Ibid., p. 257.

[14]Søren Kierkegaard, *The Present Age, and Of the Difference Between a Genius and an Apostle,* trans. Alexander Dru (New York: Harper Torchbooks, 1962), p. 103.

[15]Hatch, "Evangelicalism as a Democratic Movement," p. 12.

[16]Ibid.

[17]Barna, *Frog in the Kettle,* p. 120.

[18]Ibid., pp. 123-24.

[19]Richard Lovelace, "Evangelicalism: Recovering a Tradition of Spiritual Depth," *The Reformed Journal,* September 1990, p. 25.

**Chapter 7: In Search of Excellence**
[1]Barna, *Frog in the Kettle,* p. 150.

[2]Ibid., p. 60.

[3]Barna, *Marketing the Church,* p. 29.

[4]Philip Yancey, "The Church as Platypus," *Leadership,* Summer 1986, p. 106.

[5]Barna, *User Friendly Churches,* p. 143.

[6]Ibid., p. 153.

[7]Ibid., p. 151.

8Anderson, *Dying for Change,* p. 54.

9J. I. Packer, *A Quest for Godliness: The Puritan Vision of the Christian Life* (Wheaton, Ill.: Crossway Books, 1990), p. 22.

10Vernon Grounds, "Faith for Failure: A Meditation on Motivation for Ministry," *TSF Bulletin,* March-April 1986, p. 5.

11William Dyrness, "Aesthetics in the Old Testament: Beauty in Context," *Journal of the Evangelical Theological Society* 28 (December 1985), p. 430.

12Ibid.

13John MacArthur, Jr., *Our Sufficiency in Christ* (Dallas: Word Books, 1991), p. 152.

14Anderson, *Dying for Change,* p. 54.

15Fred Smith, "Straight Answers in a Crooked Age," *Leadership,* Summer 1983, p. 107.

16Martin Luther, *The Bondage of the Will,* trans. J. I. Packer and O. R. Johnston (Old Tappan, N.J.: Revell, 1957), p. 66.

17Grounds, "Faith for Failure," p. 5.

18Eugene Peterson, "Lashed to the Mast," *Leadership,* Summer 1986, p. 54.

## Chapter 8: The Household of Faith

1Eugene Peterson, "The Jonah Syndrome," *Leadership,* Summer 1990, p. 38.

2Eugene Peterson, "Should Christians Pay Closer Attention to the Lord's Day?" in *Tough Questions Christians Ask,* ed. David Neff (Wheaton, Ill.: Victor Books, 1989), pp. 14-15.

3Jacques Ellul, *Propaganda* (New York: Knopf, 1966), pp. 158-59.

4Cited in Packer, *Quest for Godliness,* p. 307.

5Richard Baxter, *The Reformed Pastor* (Portland, Ore.: Multnomah Press, 1982), pp. 5-7.

6Warren W. Wiersbe, *Real Worship* (Nashville: Oliver-Nelson, 1986), pp. 36-37.

7Peterson, *Long Obedience,* p. 106.

8Ibid., p. 107.

9Lesslie Newbigin, *The Gospel in a Pluralist Society* (Grand Rapids, Mich.: Eerdmans, 1989), p. 243.

10Christopher Lasch, *The True and Only Heaven: Progress and Its Critics* (New York: W. W. Norton, 1991), p. 221.

11Newbigin, *Gospel in a Pluralist Society,* p. 243.

12Baxter, *Reformed Pastor,* p. 70.